Liberal fasc:
tolerance myth

By Andy Brown

Cover design by Kev Jones

Acknowledgements

With special thanks to Dr Andrew Johnson M.B. Ch.B. who committed time to read and suggest changes to the book; without his interest and encouragement it would not have been written. Thanks also to Dr Bruce Newsome Ph.D. for his invaluable assistance in reviewing and suggesting amendments to the content; also, to Clare Johnson and Mike Barry for their support and to other friends and family members who have read the book and made helpful comments and corrections.

Introduction

Dark and sinister forces are on the rise in the United Kingdom (UK) and across the Western world; forces which seek to impose their worldview on others, which accept no dissent and which use all the powers at their disposal to silence anyone who disagrees with them. No, I'm not talking about the far-right, radical left, Islamist extremists, or government-sponsored secret services involved in some conspiracy. The forces of which I speak are more sinister, for they masquerade as champions of tolerance and liberalism. Their language is that of fairness, diversity and equality, yet they pursue an agenda which seeks to crush anyone who does not embrace their view of the world. These are the liberal fascists.

Perhaps the greatest achievement of the liberal fascists is to persuade us that they are the good guys; the custodians of tolerance, fairness, justice, progress and decency, while anyone who opposes them is intolerant, bigoted and a relic of a bygone age. This mantra is repeated time and time again by politicians, journalists, academics, activists and celebrities and appears to be generally accepted without question.

This little book is born out of concern and frustration; concern that Western society is becoming increasingly intolerant of those whose beliefs and values do not conform to the secular liberal consensus and frustration that the liberal fascists can get away with claiming to be the champions of tolerance, when they are anything but.

My aim in the following chapters is as follows: firstly, to convince you that the intolerance of the liberal fascists matters; secondly to examine what is meant by tolerance and to look at the problems that arise around this issue in diverse Western societies; thirdly to demonstrate that far from being champions of tolerance, the liberal fascists are in fact deeply intolerant and lastly, to offer some suggestions as to ways in which we might seek to be a more tolerant society.

The nature of liberal fascism will be discussed in more detail in chapter 3, but it may help the reader to offer a brief definition at this point: *"Liberal fascism is the claim to espouse liberal values, while at the same time displaying intolerant and authoritarian attitudes and behaviour towards those with whom you disagree."*

This book doesn't make any claim to be an academic research paper, but simply an observation of what is happening in the UK and other Western societies. Its approach is both philosophical and scientific. In seeking to understand the boundaries of tolerance we need to ask philosophical questions about such things as the nature of truth, good and evil, right and wrong. At the same time, when considering how tolerance is worked out in society, it is necessary to take a more scientific approach and look at the evidence for the benefit or otherwise of different courses of action.

References have been supplied for the sources of information that have been used and as such are open to anyone to check and cross-reference.

Chapter 1: Does it matter?

This short study will attempt to set out what I consider to be the 'tolerance problem' currently faced by Western society. As a result of immigration, globalisation, secularisation and technological development, the West is becoming increasingly diverse, which is making it more difficult to find shared values and to agree on the boundaries of tolerance. At the same time, those in positions of power and authority are increasingly intolerant of anyone who does not adhere to the 'liberal' values that represent the current social and political orthodoxy. While Western society is becoming more diverse, those in authority are demanding greater conformity to the 'liberal consensus'; but does it matter? Perhaps we are simply observing the inevitable march of progress and the decline of outdated and outmoded ways of thinking and believing. Maybe objections to this progress are just 'sour grapes' on the part of those who realise that their old-fashioned values are on the way out. On the other hand, could it be that the growth of intolerance is something that should concern us all, regardless of our own beliefs and values?

The value of tolerance

If we believe that tolerance is a value worth defending and fighting for, then we should be concerned about any movement, ideology or philosophy that appears to be consistently undermining it, including liberalism. A friend who helpfully reviewed an early draft of this book wrote the following:

> Brown raises some important points in Liberal Fascism & the Tolerance Myth and there is certainly a lot of food for thought in it. I'm glad that I live in a society where Brown is free to write what he thinks and that I'm not a Christian in many parts of the Middle East, gay in Chechnya or in the five countries where homosexuality is punishable by death, black in Alabama, a journalist in Egypt, living in North Korea, a burka wearer in France or a refugee fleeing Syria.

I suspect these sentiments sum up how most Western people feel about tolerance. It is something we innately value, even if we have never given the subject much consideration. We are glad, even grateful, to live in a society where for the most part people are tolerant towards one another, certainly in comparison with many other parts of the world.

However, while generally accepting the importance and benefits of tolerance, there is a tendency to ignore or overlook intolerance towards those with whom we disagree; but in the end intolerance is intolerance and if it is allowed to flourish in society then it may come back to bite us at some point in the future. In a poem called "First they came" the German Lutheran pastor Martin Niemöller (1892–1984), who emerged as a vocal public critic of Adolph Hitler, describes what happens when intolerance goes unchallenged because it doesn't affect us as individuals:

> First they came for the Socialists and I did not speak out -
> Because I was not a Socialist.
>
> Then they came for the Trade Unionists and I did not speak out -
> Because I was not a Trade Unionist.
>
> Then they came for the Jews and I did not speak out -
> Because I was not a Jew.
>
> Then they came for me and there was no one left to speak for me.[1]

It may be that having looked at the many examples of intolerance that are set out in this book, we feel little sympathy for those affected and unconcerned because it does not impact upon us at this moment in time; but who knows where this intolerance will lead if left unchallenged. If we agree with the sentiments of this poem, then we cannot afford to ignore its warning. While intolerance is at times justified, we need to be careful that we don't look the other way just because we are unsympathetic to the values of its victims. If we do, then we may find that one day we suffer a similar fate.

The importance of reason

One of the problems with intolerant world views and ideologies is that they require unquestioning adherence to a specific set of beliefs and values, even when these are shown to be harmful to individuals and wider society. Conformity is more important than truth. In the following chapters we will see that the liberal fascist's commitment to political correctness and their belief in the superiority of liberal values has led to a situation in which 'correct belief' is valued above evidence and reason, often to the detriment of society. In his book 'The Retreat of Reason', Anthony Browne, journalist, political lobbyist and author writes that:

> Political correctness is often ridiculed, but it is more than just a joke. With its earlier benefits already won, it has now become a hindrance to social progress and a threat to society. By closing down debates, it restricts the ability of society to tackle the problems that face it.[2]

In chapter 4 we will examine the impact of political correctness (PC) in more detail and see how it led to a situation in the UK where society was unable to openly debate and effectively deal with issues around race and ethnicity. We will consider the abuse of mainly white girls by predominantly Asian gangs in Rotherham and see that this happened in part because of the existence of a climate in which issues of race were too sensitive to address. Evidence and reason were jettisoned in favour of ideology and young people suffered abuse as a result. Similarly, we will see how society was unable to have a grown-up debate about the issue of mass immigration, because those who opposed it or questioned its benefits and impact were frequently accused of being motivated by racism. Trevor Phillips, the ex-chair of the Equality and Human Rights Commission, was right when he expressed the view that the well-intentioned work of that organisation in combatting racism had backfired and created a situation where people were too afraid to identify and deal with issues around race.[3]

Another example of an area where 'correct belief' takes priority over evidence is that of sexual ethics. In 2015, the Relationships Foundation, a think tank working to promote good relationships in society, calculated the cost of family breakdown to the UK taxpayer as £47 billion, which equates to £1,546 per taxpayer.[4] The Christian social reform organisation, the Jubilee Centre, which looked at all of the costs to the UK taxpayer and wider economy of sexual freedom and relationship breakdown, has estimated a figure of £100 billion annually; about twice as much as alcohol abuse, smoking and obesity combined.[5] This is just the financial cost and doesn't include the emotional and psychological impact of family breakdown and sexual freedom. Given the evidence of the negative impact of liberal sexual values on society, it would seem reasonable to ask why those in authority are not actively developing policies to address the problem. It appears that Western society prefers to hold on to its liberal beliefs regarding sexual freedom, rather than face up to the evidence of harm and modify its values and behaviour accordingly.

One last example is that of gender identity and in particular those who identify as transgender. This is a term that is used to describe people whose gender identity is not the same as, or does not sit comfortably with, the sex they were assigned at birth. The current orthodoxy is increasingly that this is a problem with the body, rather than the mind. The way to help transgender people is therefore to change their bodies to fit the way they feel, not to help individuals to 'correct' their gender identity so that it conforms to their biological sex. The process that a transgender person goes through in order to live as the gender with which they identify is known as 'transitioning'. This may take a number of forms, from simple things like changing the way they dress through to medical intervention involving the use of drugs and/or surgery.

Again, the question is whether this current orthodoxy is evidence based, or primarily driven by ideology. A number of things should give us pause for thought. Firstly, there is no scientific or medical consensus on the cause of gender dysphoria (discomfort or distress caused by a mismatch between sex assigned at birth and gender identity). If we are unsure of the cause, then presumably we should not be too dogmatic about the treatment prescribed. If it turns out that the origin is primarily psychological, then reaching for a 'physical cure' may end up doing more harm than good. Secondly the evidence for the benefit of using medical intervention (drug treatment and/or surgery) is mixed,[6] which should again lead to caution in prescribing treatments that have far reaching and long-term consequences. Thirdly, there are a growing number of people who have had gone through gender reassignment surgery, who are now seeking to have this reversed.[7] This at the very least demonstrates that physical intervention is not necessarily a panacea that solves the problems faced by those who experience gender dysphoria. Fourthly, special care has to be taken in dealing with children who express confusion or uncertainty about their gender, because the vast majority of them 'grow out of' the feelings by late adolescence.[8] This has led to some medical doctors speaking out against what is fast becoming the current orthodoxy in treating children:

> In its updated statement, Gender Dysphoria in Children (August 2016), the American College of Paediatricians calls for an end to the normalization of gender dysphoria (GD) in children because it has led to the ongoing experimentation upon, and sterilization of, confused children. Children with GD believe that they are something other than their biological sex. For children experiencing GD before the age of puberty, the confusion resolves over 80 percent of the time by late adolescence. There is a suppressed debate among professionals regarding the new

treatment "standard" for childhood GD. This media-popularized standard involves the use of medicines that block puberty followed by life-long use of toxic cross-sex hormones - a combination that results in the sterilization of minors and other significant health risks. A review of current medical literature finds this approach to be rooted in an unscientific gender ideology that violates the long-standing medical ethics principle of "First do no harm" ... Dr. Michelle Cretella, President of the College states, *"We live at a time in which social agendas often bias the results of research and lead to the development of false medical standards. Those who honourably speak out against this are chastised. Young children are being permanently sterilized and surgically maimed under the guise of treating a condition that would otherwise resolve in over 80% of them. This is criminal."*[9]

There is clearly a concern among some medical professionals that the current approach to treatment is ideologically driven rather than evidence based. Lastly, there is a wider issue with asserting that society should always validate an individual's sense of identity, even when it clearly differs from reality. Where does it end? Should we validate a white person's wish to identify as black, an able-bodied person's wish to live as if disabled, or a grown man's desire to be treated as a little girl? All these 'choices' have broader implications for society, as well as the individuals concerned.

There is also another issue, which is potentially more significant:

> Underlying the transsexual movement is a radical form of self-determination. The assumption is that a person's subjective feeling overrides objective biological reality... some of those campaigning for transsexual rights are motivated by the ideology that we should all be able to choose our own gender identity from a whole range of possibilities, without reference to biology.[10]

One key feature of modern Western society is a belief in the primacy of the individual; as John Stuart Mill, the founding father of modern Western liberalism put it: "Over himself, over his own body and mind, the individual is sovereign."[11] This belief, along with the conviction that truth is relative, means that an individual is free to choose their own gender identity, rather than being bound by the conventions of society. At this point we could just shrug our shoulders and say, 'live and let live' or 'whatever floats your boat'; but what if this ideology is harmful and damaging?

Concerns have begun to be raised about the potential impact of this new gender ideology on children and young people, the vast majority of whom have no issue with their biological gender. In July 2017, the Daily Telegraph reported that in the last five years there had been a four-fold increase in the number of children under the age of ten being referred to the NHS Gender Identity Service.[12] Some experts in the field have expressed concern that this has happened, in part, because schools are encouraging children to question their identity, as part of a politically correct agenda which is attempting to force children to 'unlearn the difference between boys and girls'. Schools are going beyond supporting 'transgender children,' to encouraging all children to question their gender identity, which is sowing confusion in children's minds, leaving many confused and traumatised.[13] This appears to be a case of creating a problem where one does not exist. Only time will tell how much damage this will do to the lives of individuals.

As we will see with other areas of liberal ideology, those who dare to question the current orthodoxy find themselves ostracised and suitably labelled, in this case as transphobic or 'anti-LGBT'. Medical professionals who dare to express an alternative viewpoint are chastised.[14] Even self-confessed liberals do not escape criticism if they are unwilling to fall into line with the accepted ideology. This was the fate of arch feminist Germaine Greer, who got into trouble with fellow liberals for suggesting that surgery couldn't change a man into a woman; trans women were not therefore 'real women'. As a result, some students at Cardiff University attempted to get her banned from speaking there in November 2015 on the basis that she had demonstrated misogynistic views towards trans women, including 'misgendering' them and denying the existence of transphobia altogether.[15]

If liberal fascism is preventing us from openly discussing and debating the problems of society and looking for solutions based on evidence and reason, rather than ideology, then it matters to all of us. Anthony Browne again helpfully comments that:

> Political correctness... is an assault on reason, because the measuring stick of the acceptability of a belief is no longer its objective, empirically established truth, but how well it fits in with the received wisdom of political correctness.[16]

The importance of truth

From the examples that we have just looked at it would seem reasonable to suggest that the liberal fascists are more concerned about 'correct belief' than they are about objective truth. This could indicate that they are not really interested in the truth at all; it is an inconvenience, to be manipulated where necessary or abandoned altogether. Alternatively, it may be that they are so convinced about the truth of their own beliefs and values that they are unwilling for them to be challenged, even when they are contradicted by the evidence. Either way the result is the same - truth is relegated to a matter of secondary importance and made subservient to the imperative to conform. It should be obvious that this is damaging. Any society that abandons a concern for truth and replaces it with dogma becomes dysfunctional and may eventually collapse under the weight of the lies it creates.

In a book called 'Everything was Forever, Until it was No More: The Last Soviet Generation', about the paradoxes of life in the Soviet Union during the 20 years before it collapsed, Alexei Yurchak professor of anthropology at the University of California, Berkeley observes that:

> Everyone knew the system was failing, but as no one could imagine any alternative to the status quo, politicians and citizens were resigned to maintaining a pretence of a functioning society. Over time, this delusion became a self-fulfilling prophecy and the "fakeness" was accepted by everyone as real, an effect that Yurchak termed "hypernormalisation".[17]

The fundamental problem was that those in authority were no longer concerned with what was true, but rather with perpetuating a lie; in this case the falsehood of the superiority of Soviet communism. While Western liberalism may seem a million miles away from Soviet authoritarianism, this book will demonstrate that similar processes are at work. The liberal fascists are not primarily concerned with discovering what is true, by examining the evidence and using reason, but rather in perpetuating the idea of the superiority of the liberal consensus. So, in chapter 4 we will see that instead of encouraging a 'desire for truth' they are seeking to close-down debate, restrict freedom of speech and supress alternative viewpoints. As in the Soviet system, what matters is that the individual conforms to a particular pattern of thinking, speaking and behaving, whether or not this has any basis in truth and whatever the consequences.

Undermining Liberal Democracy

Another reason we should be concerned about the intolerance of liberal fascism is because it undermines liberal Western democratic values. Liberal democracy is a system of government which officially recognises and protects individual rights and freedoms and limits the exercise of political power. It seeks to achieve a balance between the power of the state and the rights and freedoms of the individual. The state is given power to govern by the will of the majority, but that power is limited to ensure the rights and freedoms of the individual and protection for the minority. This is achieved through the rule of law to which both the state and individuals are subject. In addition, freedom of speech, the press and assembly are also crucial in holding the government to account and protecting the rights of individuals.

The problem with liberal fascism is that it is undermining the balance of power between the state and the individual, by increasing the power of the state over the citizen. This 'power grab' is driven by a belief in the truth of liberal values and intolerance of any ideas or beliefs that do not fit with the consensus. One example of the ambitions of the liberal fascists that we will examine in chapter 4 is the Scottish Government's attempt to bring in a scheme whereby every child has a named state guardian to look after their welfare. This was a 'power grab' that would have massively increased the influence and reach of the state over the lives of children and families, at the expense of parents. On this occasion, the 'rule of law' performed its purpose and a number of pressure groups were able to successfully challenge the government in the courts and prevent the scheme being implemented. However, we will also see many other examples where the state and its agencies are succeeding in increasing their power and influence over the lives of individuals.

As well as undermining the balance of power between the state and the individual, liberal fascism is also endangering the rights of certain minorities, by creating a situation in which some groups are favoured, promoted and protected, whilst others are marginalised. Those whose values fit with that of the liberal consensus or who are considered to be victims of past oppression are okay, but if a group's values are viewed as illiberal and it cannot make a suitable case for victimhood, it is likely to find itself marginalised. Christians of various shades appear to fall into this second category. Their traditional values are increasingly at odds with the liberal orthodoxy and any claim to be victimised is dismissed, given Christianity's historical status; this is despite the fact that practising Christians are now a small minority in Western society. The hounding of Tim Farron (the ex-leader of the Liberal Democrats) over his views on homosexuality was a good example of this. As a

Christian, he was unfortunate enough to be part of a group that harboured 'illiberal' views on human sexuality, while at the same time being unable to make an adequate claim for victimhood. As such he was considered as fair game by journalists who kept returning to his views about gay sex.[18]

Another example of the marginalisation of certain minorities is the way in which OFSTED (the Office for Standards in Education) has been seeking to impose the government's view of 'British values' on to faith schools in England. For example:

> An orthodox Jewish school has failed three Ofsted inspections because it refuses to endorse homosexuality and transsexualism, it has emerged. The Telegraph reports that Vishnitz Girls School, a private school in Hackney, North London, has consistently been marked down by Ofsted for declining to give pupils a full understanding of 'British values'. This is despite the fact that the school performs well in other areas. Over the last two years, Ofsted has faced serious criticism for its British values drive, which some feel is used to punish schools with a religious designation. Last month, Vishnitz Girls School failed its third inspection in less than a year, with Ofsted complaining that pupils are not "taught explicitly" about LGBT issues. An official report by the schools' regulator states that the school is aware of its obligation to abide by the Equality Act

2010 but chooses not to teach pupils about 'gender reassignment' and sexual orientation.[19]

Faith schools, by their very nature, derive their view of human sexuality and gender from their religion, rather than society's current values. Given that mutual tolerance and respect for those of other beliefs and faiths is a core British value[20] and that faith is also a protected characteristic under the 2010 Equality Act, you would think this would not be an issue; after all, tolerance means that we accept a diversity of belief and behaviour. If a faith school were found to be using 'religion' as a cover for teaching intolerance or inciting hatred towards others, then OFSTED would indeed be justified in challenging their understanding of British values, but in the case of the Vishnitz Girls School there was no suggestion that this was the case. Indeed, it was recognised that the school taught pupils to respect others, regardless of their beliefs or values. The school's only failing was not to teach pupils explicitly about LGBT issues. Presumably, the thinking of OFSTED is that children cannot be tolerant of the different lifestyles if they know nothing about them. This notion is fundamentally flawed. Tolerance of others is not derived from 'knowing about' every possible niche lifestyle option that exists in society, but rather from fundamental beliefs about the nature of humanity. In the case of the Judaeo-Christian perspective, people have value because they are created in the image of God and it is this belief that provides the basis for tolerating and respecting others.

Rather than the school being at fault, it appears that it is OFSTED who are confused about the nature of British values, which are not the same as, and do not require assent to the liberal orthodoxy. The idea that British values require a knowledge of and adherence to a secular liberal view of human sexuality has been 'sneaked in by the back door' and appears to be more about indoctrinating children in certain values than anything else. Assent to the acceptability of LGBT lifestyles has become the benchmark for whether or not a group or individual are tolerant. The irony is that this is a fundamentally intolerant viewpoint, which fails to recognise and respect the diversity of views that exist in society regarding human sexuality. It also demonstrates a misunderstanding of the nature of tolerance, which is not the same as agreement.

These examples demonstrate what John Stuart Mill called the tyranny of the majority. He believed that this tyranny was potentially worse than the tyranny of government:

> Where one can be protected from a tyrant, it is much harder to be protected "against the tyranny of the prevailing opinion and feeling." The prevailing opinions within society will be the basis of all rules of conduct within society; thus there can be no safeguard in law against the tyranny of the majority. Mill's proof goes as follows: the majority opinion may not be the correct opinion. The only justification for a person's preference for

a particular moral belief is that it is that person's preference. On a particular issue, people will align themselves either for or against that issue; the side of greatest volume will prevail, but is not necessarily correct.[21]

The prevailing 'opinion and feeling' in Western society is that of secular liberalism. The danger is that as the dominant worldview, this turns into a form of tyranny that crushes any minority that is unwilling or unable to sign up to its creed. The other danger is that as secular liberals are the side shouting the loudest, their worldview prevails, even though their views may not always translate into what is best for individuals and society.

To summarise, liberal democracy is undermined by liberal fascism because it increases the power of the state over the individual and discriminates against unfashionable minorities. This can lead to the 'tyranny of the majority' or of the 'prevailing opinion'. However, there is something else going on that is easily missed and arguably even more dangerous to liberal democracy – 'the tyranny of the loudest minority'.

Although it is the state which is increasing its power over the individual, this is often done at the behest of unrepresentative, vocal and fashionable minorities, who persuade the government to intervene in society to ensure that it conforms to their view of what is right. In this sense it is not the state that is taking power over the individual, as much as dominant and influential minority groups, who are acting through the state. A good example of this is the Asher's Bakery case, which we will look at in chapter 3. In this case it is the state which is eroding individual rights and freedoms through the application of the law, but government policy is being driven by powerful and vocal minorities who have successfully persuaded those in government that it is right to impose their liberal view of human sexuality on to wider society.

Another example, which we looked at earlier in this chapter, is the way transgender issues are now being introduced into schools and children encouraged to question their gender identity. This is happening despite opposition from many parents and others working in the fields of education and medicine. Once again this is being driven by a small, unrepresentative and vocal minority, who have persuaded those in government to impose their values on the rest of society. In case you think such sentiments are verging on paranoia, the British Prime Minster Theresa May said the following at the PinkNews Awards in October 2017:

> We need to keep up our action, so we are pressing ahead with inclusive relationship and sex education in English schools, making sure that LGBT issues are taught well. We're determined to eradicate homophobic and transphobic bullying... We've set out plans to reform the Gender Recognition Act, streamlining and de-medicalising the process for changing gender, because being

trans is not an illness and it shouldn't be treated as such.[22]

PinkNews covers a variety of news for the gay, lesbian, bisexual and transgender community in the UK and worldwide and as such speaks for the powerful LGBT minority, which represents approximately 3% of the UK population.[23] [24] Theresa May was the first British Prime Minister to make an appearance at the awards and was also joined by the Labour leader Jeremy Corbyn and Mayor of London Sadiq Khan. The implication appears to be that this unrepresentative and vocal minority has a significant and disproportionate influence over the direction of government policy and within British politics in general - this is the 'tyranny of the loudest minority'. These groups persuade the state to adopt their values, to which the silent majority acquiesce; those minorities that can't or won't are then marginalised and discriminated against.

Damaging social cohesion

The intolerance of the liberal fascists is also leading to a more divided and less cohesive society. Of course, this is the opposite of what is intended. PC, no platforming, safe spaces and equality and diversity policies etc., all aim to create a society that is more equal and harmonious, but the result is the opposite. The reason for this lies in the ideology of political correctness.

As we will see in chapter 4, PC is underpinned by the idea that society is divided into victims and oppressors. White men are generally seen as the oppressors and everyone else is to some extent a victim. The problem is so bad that according to David Green, in his book 'We're (nearly) all victims now', most people in the UK now fall into a group that considers itself to be victimised in some way or other.[25] He goes on to describe how this 'victim-hood' creates a divided society where groups are pitted against one another and seek to gain advantage over others through the power of the state:

> We are used to interest groups pressing their case as part of a democratic process that allows opposing views to be accommodated through reasoned discussion and compromise. But modern victim groups create entrenched social divisions by defining opponents as oppressors who must not only be defeated by the state but silenced by the state. It weakens the toleration and give and take that have been central to our political culture and even encourages aggression.[26]

The division of society into competing victim groups is also known as 'identity politics'. This is characterised by people taking up political positions that correspond to the interests and perspectives of the group to which they belong. This identity may be defined by race, religion, gender, sexual orientation or class, etc. The purpose of the group is to advance its own interests, often with little regard to the impact on others and any opposition is considered as evidence of hatred towards people of the specific identity concerned. So, for example, those who question the current orthodoxy around transgender issues are automatically labelled as transphobic or 'anti-LGBT', as if it is impossible to have an alternative viewpoint that is not driven by hatred. The impact of identity politics is that society becomes more divided and people lose the ability to engage in debate and dialogue and to disagree amicably. Ironically, the 'British values agenda', which we will refer to in the next chapter, appears to be fuelling identity politics and creating division, rather than enabling society to unite around shared values.

Yes... it matters!

The intolerance of the liberal fascists matters to us as individuals who cherish our rights and freedoms and do not wish to see them eroded. It also matters to our society, as its ideology prevents us from dealing honestly with some of the challenges we face, diminishes the importance of truth, undermines the fine balance of power that exists between the state and individuals, erodes the rights of unfashionable minorities, encourages the 'tyranny of the loudest minority' and creates a more divided and less cohesive society.

References

1. First they came (2017, May 31) In *Wikipedia, The Free Encyclopaedia*. Retrieved 19:46, August 7, 2017 from,

https://en.wikipedia.org/w/index.php?title=First_they_ca
me_...&oldid=783165807. Licenced under CC-BY-SA 3.0.
https://creativecommons.org/licenses/by-sa/3.0/

2. Browne, A., The Retreat of Reason: Political
correctness and the corruption of public debate in
modern Britain (Civitas, 2006) page xiii.

3. Mangan, L. (2015, March 20) Things we won't say
about race. The Guardian. Retrieved July 29, 2017 from
https://www.theguardian.com/tv-and-
radio/2015/mar/20/things-we-wont-say-about-race-
trevor-phillips.

4. (2015, Feb) Counting the cost of family failure.
Retrieved August 7, 2017 from
http://www.relationshipsfoundation.org/cost-of-family-
failure-47-bn-and-still-rising/.

5. Brandon, G. (2012, Jan) Free sex: who pays?
Retrieved August 7, 2017 from http://www.jubilee-
centre.org/free-sex-who-pays/.

6. McHugh, P. (2016, May 13) Transgender surgery isn't
the solution. Retrieved Jan 29, 2018 from
https://www.wsj.com/articles/paul-mchugh-transgender-
surgery-isnt-the-solution-1402615120

7. Petter, O. (2017, Oct 30) Gender reversal surgery. The
Independent. Retrieved January 29, 2018 from
http://www.independent.co.uk/life-style/gender-reversal-

surgery-demand-rise-assignment-men-women-trans-
a7980416.html

8. and 9. (2016, Aug 3) Normalizing gender dysphoria.
Retrieved July 28, 2017 from
http://www.acpeds.org/normalizing-gender-dysphoria-is-
dangerous-and-unethical.

10. (2016, Sept) Transsexualism. Retrieved July 28,
2017 from http://www.christian.org.uk/wp-
content/uploads/transsexualism2016.pdf.

11. On Liberty. (2017, July 23) In *Wikipedia, The Free
Encyclopaedia*. Retrieved 10:43, August 8, 2017 from
https://en.wikipedia.org/w/index.php?title=On_Liberty&
oldid=792009656. Licenced under CC-BY-SA 3.0.
https://creativecommons.org/licenses/by-sa/3.0/

12. and 13. Turner, C. (2017, July 8) Number of children
quadruples. Daily Telegraph. Retrieved Oct 28, 2017
from
http://www.telegraph.co.uk/news/2017/07/08/number-
children-referred-gender-identity-clinics-has-
quadrupled/

14. (2016, Aug 3) Normalizing gender dysphoria.
Retrieved July 28, 2017 from
http://www.acpeds.org/normalizing-gender-dysphoria-is-
dangerous-and-unethical.

15. Quinn, B. (2015, Oct 23) Petition urges Cardiff
University. The Guardian. Retrieved July 28, 2017 from

https://www.theguardian.com/education/2015/oct/23/petition-urges-cardiff-university-to-cancel-germain-greer-lecture.

16. Browne, A., The Retreat of Reason: Political correctness and the corruption of public debate in modern Britain (Civitas, 2006) page 5.

17. HyperNormalisation. (2017, August 31) In *Wikipedia, The Free Encyclopaedia.* Retrieved 15:29, October 28, 2017, from https://en.wikipedia.org/w/index.php?title=HyperNormalisation&oldid=798263575. Licenced under CC-BY-SA 3.0. https://creativecommons.org/licenses/by-sa/3.0/

18. Daisley, S. (2017, April 25) The cruel hounding of Tim Farron. The Spectator. Retrieved August 8, 2017 from https://blogs.spectator.co.uk/2017/04/cruel-hounding-tim-farron-bloodsport-secularists/#.

19. (2017, Jun 27) Ofsted punishes Jewish school. Retrieved August 26, 2017 from http://www.christian.org.uk/news/ofsted-punishes-jewish-school-refusing-endorse-lgbt-agenda/

20. Department of Education (2014, Nov 27) Retrieved July 28, 2017 from https://www.gov.uk/government/news/guidance-on-promoting-british-values-in-schools-published. Contains public sector information licensed under the Open Government Licence v3.0.

21. On Liberty. (2017, July 23) In *Wikipedia, The Free Encyclopaedia.* Retrieved 10:43, August 8, 2017 from https://en.wikipedia.org/w/index.php?title=On_Liberty& oldid=792009656. Licenced under CC-BY-SA 3.0. https://creativecommons.org/licenses/by-sa/3.0/

22. Duffy, N. and Jackman, J. (2017, Oct 18) Theresa May at PinkNews Awards. Retrieved Nov 22, 2017 from http://www.pinknews.co.uk/2017/10/18/prime-minister-theresa-may-addresses-pinknews-awards/

23. (2016, Jan). Transgender Equality. First Report of Session 2015-2016. Retrieved August 26, 2017 from https://publications.parliament.uk/pa/cm201516/cmselec t/cmwomeq/390/390.pdf

24. (2016, Oct 5) Sexual identity: UK 2015. Retrieved August 7, 2017 from https://www.ons.gov.uk/peoplepopulationandcommunity/ culturalidentity/sexuality/bulletins/sexualidentityuk/201 5. Contains public sector information licensed under the Open Government Licence v3.0.

25. Green, G., We're (nearly) all victims now! (Civitas, 2006) page 7.

26. Green, G., We're (nearly) all victims now! (Civitas, 2006) page 2-3

Chapter 2: Tolerance

What is tolerance?

Tolerance is: $\left(\text{COWARDICE} \right) \left(\text{WEAKNESS} \right)$

A willingness to accept behaviour and beliefs that are different from your own, although you might not agree with or approve of them.[1]

Someone who is tolerant is by definition willing to accept that others behave or think differently than they do. Additionally, tolerance also implies allowing alternative beliefs or practises to exist without interference. Real tolerance isn't just about permitting other people to think or believe something (how could you stop them anyway?), it is also about allowing them to live out and express those beliefs or values.

Tolerance is essentially to do with how we handle disagreement. If people share our views, then we don't need to tolerate them; the issue only arises when we think others are wrong. This basic understanding of the nature of tolerance seems to have been lost in modern Western society. Nowadays if you think that someone is wrong, you are likely to be branded as intolerant, but tolerance is not about agreeing with other people, it is more to do with how disagreements are handled and expressed.

Having defined what tolerance is, several things become fairly self-evident. Firstly, tolerance is not universally accepted as something good or desirable, even in Western society. Islamists and those on the extremes of the political right and left do not believe in tolerance, rather they see intolerance of their enemies or opponents as a virtue. However, this isn't just a problem of extremism; you don't have to look too hard in wider society to find intolerant attitudes being expressed. This is particularly true on the internet, where we have seen the rise of so-called 'internet trolls'. These individuals appear to go out of their way to post provocative, offensive and inflammatory material on forums, blogs and in chat rooms. More widely, the anonymity of the internet appears to encourage the expression of intolerant and unpleasant opinions. However, it would hardly be contentious to suggest that Western societies generally see tolerance as something that is good and a value that should be promoted. Indeed, as we shall see, the UK government has stated that tolerance is a key British value.[2]

Secondly, no one is completely tolerant. There are certain things which most people, at least in the Western world, would agree should not be tolerated: domestic violence, modern-day slavery, racism, fraud, murder, theft, paedophilia and drink-driving etc. Tolerance is not a blank cheque and intolerance is not always a bad thing. Society would be very ugly if we were to tolerate all the excesses of human behaviour and belief. The line must be drawn somewhere and in most cases it is obvious why, as a society, we are intolerant of certain behaviours and beliefs. The purpose of the law, at least in part, is to establish the boundaries of tolerance and to enforce those limits.

Thirdly, while there may be considerable agreement in Western society about what behaviours and beliefs are acceptable or unacceptable, there are also many areas where disagreement exists. These sometimes fundamental differences of opinion range across a whole plethora of issues from the moral and ethical, through to those of politics, social policy and the environment. Abortion, human sexuality, pornography, same-sex marriage, gender identity, euthanasia, climate change, tax avoidance, immigration, civil liberties and terrorism are just some of the issues where people will express quite different views about what should be tolerated. Different attitudes to these issues are driven by a variety of factors including: culture, religion, worldview (outlook on life and basic beliefs), age, level of education, class and political affiliation, etc.

The tolerance problem

Given that tolerance has its limits and that there are many issues where people will have different opinions, we need to ask a difficult question, i.e. what beliefs and behaviours should we tolerate as a society and of what should we be intolerant? Where societies are largely homogenous and most people share the same culture and worldview, this can be relatively straightforward;

everyone is essentially coming from the same place, or as they say, 'singing from the same hymn sheet'. However, the Western world is now far more diverse and this means that it is more difficult to find shared values and to establish the boundaries of tolerance.

Immigration and globalisation LEFTWING TACTIC TO DESTROY WESTERN NATIONS

The most obvious reason for increased diversity in Western society is mass immigration and globalisation. People have come to the West from all over the world as refugees, asylum seekers, students and workers and they have brought with them their own cultures, religions and worldviews. While immigration to the UK has occurred throughout its history, the numbers coming have increased quite significantly since the Second World War. The UK census in 2011 showed that 13% of the population of England and Wales were born outside the country, compared to 4.3% in 1951.[3] Immigration may bring benefits but it also creates challenges, especially when those arriving have beliefs and values that differ from those of the host society. We will examine this issue in more detail in chapter 5, when we look at the subject of multiculturalism. LEFTWING CRIME

PROBLEMS

Globalisation and technological development has also made the world smaller and more interconnected. Different countries and continents are only hours away by plane. Mobile phones and the internet allow people to encounter and explore different values and beliefs in ways that would not have been possible in the past.

Islamists and other extremists have been quick to pick up on and exploit these opportunities and the use of the internet to promote their ideologies is now a major concern for Western governments.[4] Values that differ from mainstream society can be broadcast from anywhere in the world and encountered and embraced by individuals in the privacy of their own homes.

Secularisation

The difficulty in finding shared values is not just a product of immigration, globalisation and technological development, but is also due to changes that have taken place within Western culture. In the past, this culture shared a basic worldview that could be described as Judaeo-Christian, with all that flowed from that in terms of behaviour and belief, but this is no longer true. The West is now post-Christian and the predominant worldview is that of secularism. Technically speaking, secularism is simply to do with the separation of the state from religious institutions, but it has come to describe a general worldview that exists without reference to religion. Unlike the Judaeo-Christian worldview, secularism doesn't have an overarching and clearly articulated narrative or set of values that the average man or woman in the street could describe or sign up to. Most people who have a secular worldview have never thought about the fact that they adhere to a belief system and couldn't describe in any clear sense what its values are. They have simply absorbed the morality of the society around them. When secular values are articulated, they are often couched in vague terms like fairness, equality and tolerance, which mean different things to different people. The fact that the UK government has felt it necessary to try to define British values is indicative of the problem. At the very least, it suggests a society that is somewhat unclear and divided about what it believes.

Culture wars

The other impact of increasing secularisation is the conflict it creates between those who hold secular, 'progressive' and socially liberal values and those adhering to more traditional, conservative and faith-based worldviews. This 'culture war', as it has been described, is hardly surprising given that these two groups have very different underlying beliefs and assumptions. For secularists, it is human beings that make the rules and define the values by which society operates; these are not fixed and can change over time as society develops. For those who have a religious faith, it is God or gods who ultimately set the rules and define what is good and bad, right or wrong. While the application of these 'divine laws' may vary over time, human beings are not at liberty to change the rules just because they don't like them. People of faith therefore find themselves in a situation where they are unable or unwilling to modify their beliefs to fit in with the changing attitudes of secular society.

The conflict between these two very different worldviews is particularly stark in the United States, where it has been one of the stories of American politics over the last few decades and of the election of Donald Trump as US President in January 2017. In general terms, those with a secular mind-set are more likely to support the Democrats and those with a religious mind-set more likely to back the Republicans.[5] There seems to be little chance at present of these two groups uniting around shared values. A similar clash of worldviews is also occurring in the UK, although it doesn't have the same political dimension as in the US. While British society is increasingly liberal in its social attitudes,[6] those who have a religious faith are generally more socially conservative[7] and sometimes have attitudes and beliefs that do not sit comfortably with the wider society. The same story of growing secularisation is occurring throughout the Western world[8] and the overall result of these trends is a situation in which there are a significant minority of people in Western societies who do not share the increasingly liberal and secular values of the majority.

For the sake of clarity, it is perhaps worth saying that this conflict is not inevitable. Secularism should essentially be benign and neutral in that it denies privilege to religion of any type (including 'secular religions' such as humanism) but goes no further in restricting it. The American constitution is an example of this approach, in that while it separates church and state, it also guarantees freedom of belief. However, we will see that there appears to be a trend in Western society towards the privatising of religion and the exclusion of faith from the public space. This goes beyond the secular concern that religion should not have a privileged position in society and appears to be leading to a situation in which people holding faith-based values are both silenced and discriminated against. Conversely, 'secular religion' is being promoted and given a place of privilege. This is a denial of the principles of liberty and equality, as well as of the liberal notion of the secular state, which should not give preference to any belief system or worldview.

A lack of shared values

Increasing cultural diversity inevitably means that Western society is more divided in its values and beliefs. At the same time, secularisation has led to a situation where people are less clear about what they believe and why they believe it. There is also a growing division between those who hold secular and faith-based worldviews. As a result, it is difficult to see how Western countries can meaningfully talk about finding shared values, without expressing them in such vague terms as to render them almost meaningless. While we can all sign up to values such as tolerance, fairness and equality, we soon run into difficulties when we start to think about what these mean in practice. For example, British values are supposed to include a belief in mutual tolerance and respect for those of other beliefs and faiths,[9] but what happens when the expression of religious freedom appears to lead to discrimination, or when the demand for equality tramples on the conscience of another person?

So here we see the tolerance problem - given a lack of shared values, how do we decide of what we should be intolerant? If we are not all 'singing from the same hymn sheet', who decides on the words and the tune? In most mundane aspects of everyday life this is not too much of a problem as the limits of tolerance are generally accepted and understood, but what happens when this is not the case? This is particularly problematic in the areas of ethics, morality and certain cultural values and practices that are accepted within some groups, but not in others.

References

1. The Online Cambridge Dictionary; 2017. Retrieved July 28, 2017 from http://dictionary.cambridge.org/dictionary/english/Tolerance.

2. Department of Education (2014, Nov 27) Retrieved July 28, 2017 from https://www.gov.uk/government/news/guidance-on-promoting-british-values-in-schools-published. Contains public sector information licensed under the Open Government Licence v3.0.

3. 2011 Census analysis (2013, Dec 17) Retrieved July 28, 2017 from

https://www.ons.gov.uk/peoplepopulationandcommunity/
populationandmigration/internationalmigration/articles/
immigrationpatternsofnonukbornpopulationsinenglanda
ndwalesin2011/2013-12-17. Contains public sector
information licensed under the Open Government
Licence v3.0.

4. Mughal, S. (2016, April 8) Radicalisation of young
people through social media. Retrieved July 28, 2017
from https://www.internetmatters.org/hub/expert-
opinion/radicalisation-of-young-people-through-social-
media.

5. Smith, G. and Martinez, J. (2016, Nov 9) How the
faithful voted. Retrieved July 28, 2017 from
http://www.pewresearch.org/fact-tank/2016/11/09/how-
the-faithful-voted-a-preliminary-2016-analysis.

6. Harding, R. Key findings. Retrieved July 28, 2017
from http://www.bsa.natcen.ac.uk/latest-report/british-
social-attitudes-34/key-findings/context.aspx.

7. British social attitudes 34 – moral issues. Retrieved
July 28, 2017 from
http://www.bsa.natcen.ac.uk/media/39147/bsa34_moral_
issues_final.pdf. page 2.

8. Tice, D.J. (2016, April 15) While West grows secular.
Retrieved August 29, 2017 from
http://www.startribune.com/while-west-grows-secular-
the-world-gets-religion/375906371/

9. Department for Education (2014, Nov 27) Retrieved July 28, 2017 from https://www.gov.uk/government/news/guidance-on-promoting-british-values-in-schools-published. Contains public sector information licensed under the Open Government Licence v3.0.

Chapter 3: The liberal fascists

If you are a liberal fascist, then the answer to the tolerance problem as outlined in the previous chapter is quite simple. There are a set of liberal values that are ~THAT IS~ self-evidently true and superior to any others and which ~HAPPENING~ therefore need to be 'imposed' upon society. <u>Those who reject these values are to be marginalised and silenced, both for their own good and the benefit of wider society.</u> Given the existence of these superior values, it is not necessary to debate the issue of tolerance or to seek to find some middle ground between competing groups and ideas; after all, it is the liberals who are 'progressive' and 'modern' and in that case probably right as well. You may not hear liberals putting it quite so bluntly, but the evidence provided in this chapter and the next will demonstrate that this is what they actually believe.

Who are the liberal fascists?

So, who is this group of people that have been labelled as the 'liberal fascists'? How is it possible to even use these two words together when one is surely the opposite of the other? Before answering that question let's try to define what we mean by liberal fascism.

'Liberalism' is a political philosophy or worldview, the origins of which can be traced as far back as the Greek philosopher Plato. However, the modern liberal movement emerged in 17th century Europe, the father of which is generally agreed to be John Locke (1632-1704).[1]

At the heart of liberalism is a belief in the pre-eminence of the individual.[2] It is the individual that is the most important component of society and it is for their benefit that society should primarily be organised. In this sense liberalism emphasises the individual over the collective. For people to flourish and fulfil their potential certain enablers are essential, namely liberty and equality. From these flow other liberal ideas such as tolerance, freedom of religion, the separation of church and state, freedom of speech and assembly, individual rights and government by consent. While liberalism contains many different sub groups, including libertarians, neo-liberals, conservative liberals and cultural liberals, etc., there is a general agreement that it can be divided into the two main forms of classical and social liberalism.

Classical liberalism emerged during what has been termed the Age of Enlightenment, in 17th and 18th century Europe. It rejected the prevailing social and political structures of hereditary privilege, state religion, absolute monarchy and the divine right of kings. These structures gave the state enormous power over the individual, which was often abused. They also limited the potential of the individual to flourish and prosper, as the ability to do so depended on status and privilege, which was fundamentally inequitable. In response to this, the classical liberals emphasised individual liberty and sought to reduce and restrict the role of the state, believing that freedom and liberty produced the best opportunity for individual fulfilment.

The right to be free from unnecessary state interference was paramount.

Social liberalism developed during the 19th century as a response to the problems that arose from industrialisation and urbanisation. While these processes gave individuals great opportunities, they also led to significant problems such as poverty, exploitation, wealth inequality and economic uncertainty. While still believing in individualism and liberty, the social liberals believed that the state should play a positive role in helping the individual to prosper and fulfil their potential. Rather than limit the role of the state they sought to increase it, with the aim of creating a 'level playing field' and giving individuals equal access to opportunity. For example, if some individuals did not have access to education or health care, then they could not fulfil their potential in the same way as those who did. The state therefore needed to intervene to ensure that they had that opportunity, by providing education and health care for all its citizens. The implementation of these ideas in the Liberal welfare reforms of 1906-1914 led to the beginning of the welfare state in the UK.

Without being too simplistic, we could say that classical liberalism promoted individual liberty by reducing the power of the state, while social liberalism sought the same goal by increasing that power. Both were concerned with enabling the individual to flourish and fulfil their potential, but they differed as to how to achieve it. The ideology of social liberalism has had a significant influence on most of the social democratic parties in the West, whether conservative or socialist[3] and it is now the dominant form of liberalism.

Before moving on we need to briefly consider a couple of other aspects of liberalism. The reader may have noticed that we have already used the word 'liberal' in two different ways; firstly, to refer to 'liberal social attitudes' (chapter 2) and secondly to describe a particular philosophy. While the two are clearly related (liberal social attitudes originate from a philosophy that prioritises individual liberty, rights and social justice, etc.), it is necessary to make a distinction between them. When we talk about British society becoming more liberal in its social attitudes, we don't mean that most people in the UK ascribe to or understand liberalism at a philosophical level, rather we mean that they have absorbed the liberal values that are currently dominant among those who wield power and influence in the culture. It is possible to have socially liberal attitudes, while holding a wide variety of political views.

We also need to revisit the relationship between liberalism and secularism, which we have already mentioned in chapter 2. Classical liberalism was born during the Enlightenment and although many of the influential thinkers of the time, such as John Locke, did not abandon belief in God, the period marked a movement away from religion as the ultimate source of knowledge. This was replaced with rationalism (human reason), empiricism (verifiable knowledge acquired through the senses and experience) and a belief in human autonomy. By the time we get to influential liberal thinkers such as Jeremy Bentham (1748-1832) and John Stuart Mill (1806-1873), this movement away from 'traditional' religion was more advanced. Belief in a transcendent God had been replaced with the new 'religion of humanity'; what we now call secular humanism.[4] This worldview did away with 'superstitious beliefs' about God and personal salvation and focused instead on 'salvation' in the here and now. It replaced God with humanity.

It would probably be fair to say that while liberalism does not have to be secular in its outlook, it is now overwhelmingly so. However, it would be too simplistic to suggest that the issue of tolerance in Western society is primarily located in a clash between liberal secularism and conservative religion. At the heart of liberalism is a belief in the priority of individual liberty and freedom. While believing that the state should be secular and that no religion should have a place of privilege, true liberals are also committed to the idea of tolerance and religious freedom. Liberalism, secularism and religion are not necessarily incompatible.

Tolerance, liberty, equality, social justice and human rights are all things which I suspect most of us value and would wish to see promoted in society. In addition, liberal political movements have made significant positive contributions to Western society in the past and continue to do so to this day. In the light of these considerations, the use of the term 'liberal fascism' should not be seen as an attack on liberalism in general; however, as someone said to me recently, "Good old-fashioned liberalism seems to have morphed into something altogether less attractive." Anthony Browne puts it like this:

> Liberals of earlier generations accepted unorthodoxy as normal. Indeed, the right to differ was a datum (*assumption*) of classical liberalism. The Politically Correct do not give that right a high priority. It distresses their programmed minds. Those who do not conform should be ignored, silenced or vilified.[5]

This leads conveniently to the subject of fascism. It should be obvious from the context that the term 'fascism' is being used here in its informal sense, i.e. not to describe a political philosophy, but rather a way of believing and behaving. Fascists, in this sense, are people who are intolerant of alternative views and opinions; variant thought is unacceptable. In the case of liberal fascists, this intolerance is of views, opinions and beliefs that do not conform to the current political and moral orthodoxy. Additionally, fascists are also by instinct authoritarian and will use their power to coerce others to accept their beliefs and values.[6]

This chapter and the next will show that many of the individuals and groups who claim to be liberal and above all tolerant are in fact anything but. We will see that the liberal fascists deny the basic core liberal principles of liberty and equality and that the tolerance they often speak of is a myth. One cannot claim to be a champion of tolerance, while actively behaving in a way that is intolerant; this is both hypocritical and dishonest. In terms of a working definition: *"Liberal fascism is the claim to espouse liberal values, while at the same time displaying intolerant and authoritarian attitudes and behaviour towards those with whom you disagree."* It is something that only becomes apparent through the use – or perhaps we should say 'abuse' – of power.

Before looking at a few examples, let me make a couple of general points. Firstly, the reader is left to decide who fits into the group. If any names of individuals or organisations are mentioned, it is only because they appear to display the characteristics of liberal fascism; it is up to you to decide whether you agree. Secondly, I didn't invent the phrase. In discussing the issue of liberalism and intolerance with others over the last few years, many have used the term 'fascist' to describe the way in which so-called liberals sometimes behave and it is this which gave rise to the term 'liberal fascism'. It has subsequently come to my attention that the phrase has also been used by Jonah Goldberg, in the title of his book on the history of the American Left.[7]

I am also aware that the word 'fascism' has been somewhat devalued and that it is often used as a term of abuse or simply to refer to those who are authoritarian; however, its use here is justified in that it highlights the contradiction that frequently exists between the claims and actions of people who have liberal views. Those who are the most vociferous in their opposition to fascism, are frequently adopting the same attitudes and behaviours as those they condemn.

Champions of tolerance

Before giving some examples of what I have called 'liberal fascism', we should perhaps look at how some of the people and organisations I am going to mention view themselves in relation to the concept of tolerance. At the time of writing, the strap line on the Liberal Democrat's website was, "The only party fighting to keep Britain open, tolerant and united." Interestingly they are one of the few UK political parties to specifically express a belief in tolerance as a core value; though perhaps this should not surprise us as they are the only mainstream party to directly appeal to liberalism as underpinning their values.

The Conservative government, under the leadership of David Cameron and then Theresa May, included tolerance of those of different faiths and beliefs as one of the key values which it believed should characterise British society.[8] This emphasis on tolerance should not surprise us, as under David Cameron's leadership a concerted effort was made to 'detoxify' the Conservative Party[9] and transform it into a more modern, liberal and 'compassionate' political party, ditching any lingering attachment to conservative social values. The clearest example of this was the championing of the cause of gay marriage. It is perhaps worth saying that the launch of the idea of British values occurred during the Conservative-Liberal Democrat coalition (2010-2015); though the Conservatives have since pursued the idea enthusiastically.

When this book was being written, the other main UK political parties of the liberal left, such as the Greens, Labour and the Scottish National Party, did not specifically refer to tolerance as a core value on their websites; however, they all stressed values and set out policies which implied a commitment to it. Fairness, non-discrimination, equality, diversity, inclusion and social justice cannot exist without tolerance. However, the best indication of the value they place on tolerance is their very public opposition to those they believe to be intolerant, especially anyone deemed to be racist, Islamophobic or homophobic, etc. For example, in its 2017 manifesto the Labour Party describes itself as the party of equality, seeking to build a world free of racism, anti-Semitism and Islamophobia.[10] In this sense, their belief in tolerance is very clearly implied.

Political attitudes to the issue of tolerance don't just remain in that sphere, but through legislation and other means filter down to impact on all the other institutions of society. As we examine the issue of tolerance we will see that secular liberal values are firmly entrenched throughout the public and private sectors, in government, education, the criminal justice system, health care, private businesses and the charity sector etc. An example of the dominance of liberal attitudes appeared in a report by the Adam Smith Institute in March 2017 entitled 'Lackademia', which found that there was a significant liberal-left bias in British Universities. When compared with the general public, far less academics supported conservative or right-wing parties.[11]

Some examples of liberal fascism

The first three examples of liberal fascism all revolve around a common theme – the use of the words 'bigot' or 'bigoted', which means intolerance of those who hold a different opinion. This is one of liberal fascist's favourite words, which they frequently use to label and dismiss those who don't share their views. The first example occurred when the coalition government under David Cameron was pushing the gay marriage legislation through parliament in 2012. The Deputy Prime Minister Nick Clegg was due to make a speech to supporters of gay marriage and according to the text released by his office planned to denounce opponents of same-sex marriage as 'bigots'.[12] The alleged plan to use the word led to uproar and it is claimed the text of the speech was hastily changed. Of course, the irony of this should be immediately obvious; bigotry is intolerance towards people who hold a different opinion and if Nick Clegg did intend to use the word, it demonstrated his own intolerance towards those who opposed gay marriage. While this may be understandable, given that he believed in the cause of 'equal marriage', the problem is that as a Liberal Democrat he also claimed to be committed to tolerance. Remember that tolerance is the ability or willingness to tolerate the existence of opinions or behaviour that you dislike or disagree with, not just the ones you happen to like. The other problem with the alleged use of the word bigot, was that its use was unjustified in this context. Those opposed to gay marriage represented a large group with complex reasons for their opposition, which went beyond simple bigotry. Over 500,000 people signed a petition against the legislation and they were motivated by a variety of reasons, including the religious conviction that marriage is a divine institution, rather than a human construct.[13] The use of the word 'bigot' in this situation was a classic case of 'reductionism' – reducing the complexity of an issue to an over-simplification.

A second example is the now notorious incident during the 2010 election campaign when Gordon Brown, the then leader of the Labour Party, was overheard calling a member of the public a 'bigoted woman'.[14] Gillian Duffy, a lifelong Labour voter, had challenged Gordon Brown on issues of crime and immigration and when he got back into his car he was still wearing a broadcast microphone and was heard to make the comments. Again, this little incident reveals much about the mentality of the liberal fascists. The view was widely held on the political left that anyone who raised issues about immigration was essentially racist,[15] therefore by definition 'bigoted' and certainly not worth having a conversation with; a view which seems to prevail in the minds of many liberals to this day. In this case no attempt was made to understand the viewpoint of Gillian Duffy, which was just dismissed. Once more the irony is obvious. The Labour Party claims to believe in tolerance, which implies at least a modicum of open mindedness, but Gordon Brown's response to Gillian Duffy spoke only of intolerance and a closed mind. As with Nick Clegg, he had also fallen into the trap of reductionism – reducing complex and justifiable concerns around crime and immigration to bigotry.

The last example occurred more recently. In June 2017, the Conservative Party led by Theresa May won the British general election but lost their overall parliamentary majority. As a result, they announced that they were looking to gain the support of the Democratic Unionist Party to give them the votes they needed to govern. The DUP is a unionist party based in Northern Ireland and is known for being socially conservative. The liberal left was in apoplexy at the thought of such an arrangement and accused the DUP of all kinds of bigotry.[16] It clearly didn't occur to them that not everyone shared their 'self-evidently true' liberal values and that the DUP's social conservatism might resonate with many people in the UK. As all the main political parties have embraced liberal values, the millions of voters who are socially conservative have effectively found themselves disenfranchised, with no one to represent their views. In addition, the liberals' reaction appeared to overlook that fact that these 'bigots' won the most votes in Northern Ireland and so had a democratic mandate. As such they represented part of the political spectrum and of the electorate and so had the right to have their voice heard. Again, as with the previous two cases, the liberals were guilty of reducing a complex issue (the DUP and its supporters) to one word – bigotry.

The use of the word 'bigot' in all of these instances tells us much about the liberal fascist mind-set. Primarily it demonstrates intolerance towards those who hold alternative views. If you don't agree with the liberal consensus then you are a bigot, to be condemned and vilified, rather than someone who has a different opinion, to be understood, engaged with and maybe even respected. It also indicates an inherent sense of superiority and arrogance; liberal values are self-evidently true so there is no need to listen to those who have a different perspective. Furthermore, it speaks of intellectual laziness. It is easier to brand your opponents as bigots than to make any attempt to see things from their perspective or think through the issues involved. Simply taking the 'correct' moral high ground is all that is required, the additional benefit being that you don't need to worry about the possible shortcomings of your own position. Perhaps the worst thing about the use of such language is that its purpose is to demonise those with whom you disagree, which is a very fascist trait!

The first three examples have focused on the way in which the liberal fascists claim to believe in tolerance and yet behave in a way which is obviously intolerant, but how do they use their power to coerce others to accept their beliefs and values? We will return to this later in the next chapter looking at the tactics of the liberal fascists, but one of the main ways in which they seek to force their views on others is by using the power of the state.

One example of this is the UK government's attempt to define British values, which it is seeking to impose through various instruments of the state, including the education system and the courts. This is in large part driven by the issues of Islamist and far right extremism and therefore the need to define British values in terms which clearly oppose extremist ideologies. According to the government the four core British values are democracy, the rule of law, individual liberty and mutual respect and tolerance of those with different faiths and beliefs.[17] This sounds great until we start to dig a little deeper and discover that in practice tolerance means accepting the liberal views of the largely secular ruling elite and that respect for those of different faiths and beliefs means little if they happen to clash with the latest orthodoxy.

A good example of this attitude came to light when Britain's equalities czar at the time, Dame Louise Casey DBE CB, gave oral evidence to the Commons Communities Committee on January 9th 2017, following a government review on opportunity and integration of isolated communities, She equated Christian schools with extremists for teaching that marriage is between a man and a woman and claimed that Catholic schools were 'homophobic.' Casey said:

> "It is not okay for Catholic schools to be homophobic and anti-gay marriage. That is not okay either – it is not how we bring children up in this country. It is often veiled as religious conservatism and I have a problem with the expression 'religious conservatism,' because often it can be anti-equalities."[18]

The implication seems to be that while tolerance of others' beliefs is a core British value, the authorities are in fact intolerant of values that do not fit with the current liberal orthodoxy. A traditional view of marriage is not a valid alternative viewpoint, but rather an indication of homophobia. In addition, Casey's comments suggest that those in authority have in mind their own hierarchy of values and rights in which equality is at the top. Tolerance only goes so far when a conflict emerges between the equality agenda and religious belief, though it is hard to see the logic behind such an approach. Why should someone's right to believe and express the view that marriage is between a man and a woman, be considered any less important than the right of same sex couples to marry?

We have already seen cases in the UK where people have been taken to court for the perceived breaking of equality laws and successfully prosecuted, even though their actions were motivated by their beliefs, which according to our British values should be respected and tolerated. A good example of this is the Asher's Bakery case. This involved a Christian bakery company in Northern Ireland. The company was asked to provide a cake with the slogan 'Support Gay Marriage' written on it. The company refused, because although happy to provide the cake, the slogan would promote a view contrary to their religious beliefs. The customer, Mr. Lee, then complained to the Equality Commission who brought a case of discrimination against Asher's Bakery on the grounds of Mr. Lee's sexual orientation; he was gay. In 2016 the Court found against the bakery although it became clear that the bakers neither knew nor asked about the sexual orientation of the customer. In other words, the bakery didn't discriminate against Mr. Lee because he was gay but refused his request because they objected to the message he wanted on the cake. Commenting on the case and supporting the Court's ruling, the UK Government's minister responsible for faith and integration, Lord Bourne, told Premier Radio there should be "no hatred on the basis of sexual orientation."[19] This demonstrated the perverse thinking of the authorities that an objection to gay marriage equated to a hatred of gay people. It also misrepresented the facts of the case and set a worrying precedent. The logical outcome is that anyone providing services could be forced to do something that goes against their values. For example, a Muslim printer could be legally obliged to produce a book with pictures of Mohammed in it.

In the Asher's case, it appeared that mutual respect and tolerance for those of different faiths and beliefs was in short supply. The perceived crime against equality was considered more important than the rights of an individual to live according to their beliefs and conscience or to disagree with the current social or political orthodoxy. The inherent problem with this artificial hierarchy of rights was picked up by the veteran gay rights campaigner Peter Tatchell, who while initially supporting the action against Asher's Bakery, subsequently changed his mind because of the impact of the court ruling on freedom of conscience, speech and religion.[20]

Similar intolerance of people expressing views that are at odds with the liberal consensus is found in organisations throughout the public and private sectors. One such example is that of Gary McFarlane, an experienced relationships counsellor, who was dismissed for gross misconduct after indicating during a training course that he might have a conscientious objection to providing sex therapy to same-sex couples:

> Gary worked as a relationships counsellor with Relate Avon Ltd for over four years and had a good working relationship with his colleagues. During this time, he began training in a specific form of sex therapy known as 'psycho-sexual therapy' (PST). He told his supervisor that, on account of

his Christian faith, he may be unable to provide such therapy to a same-sex couple. As a result, he was dismissed instantly for gross misconduct for allegedly breaching the company's 'equality and diversity' policy. Gary had not yet been asked to provide PST to a same-sex couple in practice and had the situation ever arisen, his beliefs could have been accommodated without the risk of anyone being denied a service.[21]

The tolerance myth

The liberal fascists claim to be committed to tolerance and in the UK the authorities have gone as far as to state that it is a core British value, but in practice they often appear intolerant of anyone who does not share their liberal values. They are also increasingly using the law, the courts, education and other arms of the state to impose their liberal views on to the rest of society. While claiming to promote tolerance of different faiths and beliefs, their emphasis on equality is restricting freedom of religion, speech and conscience. Ultimately the much-vaunted tolerance of the liberal fascists is in fact a myth; a widely held but false belief. Their tolerance only stretches to beliefs and opinions that they find acceptable.

We ought to go further and suggest that the actions of the liberal fascists demonstrate that they are not liberal at all. They do not believe in equality, for they seek to advance the interests of some groups over others. They do not believe in individual liberty, for they consistently increase the influence and control of the state over the lives of the individual. They have gone beyond the desire of the social liberals to 'create a level playing field' where all have equal access to opportunity and have entered the territory of fascism, dictating to individuals what they should believe, think and say. They have also strayed from true liberalism in that they are more concerned with dogma than objective, empirically established truth. Reason has been abandoned in favour of ideology. *"It is dangerous to be right when your government is wrong" Voltaire*

References

1. John Locke. (2017, December 29). In *Wikipedia, The Free Encyclopaedia*. Retrieved 09:32, January 4, 2018, from https://en.wikipedia.org/w/index.php?title=John_Locke&oldid=817585986 Licenced under CC-BY-SA 3.0. https://creativecommons.org/licenses/by-sa/3.0/

2. Individualism. Retrieved Jan 4, 2018 from https://www.tutor2u.net/politics/reference/individualism-liberalism

3. Social liberalism. (2017, December 11). In *Wikipedia, The Free Encyclopaedia*. Retrieved 10:57, December 19, 2017, from https://en.wikipedia.org/w/index.php?title=Social_liberalism&oldid=814911229 Licenced under CC-BY-SA 3.0. https://creativecommons.org/licenses/by-sa/3.0/

4.Raeder, L.C. (2001) Mill's Religion of Humanity. Retrieved Dec 15, 2017 from page http://www.nhinet.org/raeder14-2.pdf. pg12ff.

5. Browne, A. The Retreat of Reason: Political correctness and the corruption of public debate in modern Britain (Civitas, 2006) page 2.

6. Forsyth, F. (2011, Feb 11) Fascism didn't go. The Daily Express. Retrieved July 20, 2017 from http://www.express.co.uk/comment/columnists/frederick-forsyth/228446/Fascism-didn-t-go-it-found-another-name.

7. Liberal Fascism. (2017, July 27) In *Wikipedia, The Free Encyclopaedia*. Retrieved16:15, October 13, 2017, from, https://en.wikipedia.org/w/index.php?title=Liberal_Fascism&oldid=792640459

8. Department of Education (2014, Nov 27) Retrieved July 28, 2017 from https://www.gov.uk/government/news/guidance-on-promoting-british-values-in-schools-published. Contains public sector information licensed under the Open Government Licence v3.0.

9. Watt, N. (2012, Sept 11) Stop detoxifying. The Guardian. Retrieved Oct 30, 2017 from https://www.theguardian.com/politics/2012/sep/11/tory-group-cameron-detoxifying-values

10. Labour Party Manifesto. Retrieved Oct 30, 2017 from https://labour.org.uk/manifesto/a-more-equal-society/#fourth

11. Noah, C. (2017, March 2) Lackademia. Retrieved October 13, 2017 from https://www.adamsmith.org/research/lackademia-why-do-academics-lean-left

12. Kirkup, J. (2012, Sep 11) The Daily Telegraph. Retrieved July 28, 2017 from http://www.telegraph.co.uk/news/politics/nick-clegg/9536368/Nick-Cleggs-office-attempts-to-withdraw-bigot-comment-about-opponents-of-gay-marriage.html.

13. Connor, L. (2012, June 12) Anti-gay marriage petition. The Independent. Retrieved Oct 30, 2017 from http://www.independent.co.uk/news/uk/home-news/david-cameron-presented-with-anti-gay-marriage-petition-signed-by-500000-7844717.html

14. Prince, R. (2010, April 28) Gordon Brown. Daily Telegraph. Retrieved Nov 28, 2017 from http://www.telegraph.co.uk/news/election-2010/7645072/Gordon-Brown-calls-campaigner-bigoted-woman.html

15. Lawes, S. (2013, Nov 29) Concerns about immigration. Retrieved Oct 13, 2017 from http://www.politics.co.uk/comment-analysis/2013/11/29/comment-racism-ruins-the-anti-immigration-debate

16. Jones, O. (2015, April 24) Never mind the SNP. The Guardian. Retrieved July 28. 2017 from https://www.theguardian.com/commentisfree/2015/apr/24/snp-dup-democratic-unionist-party-government-tories-anti-scottish-coalition-homophobic.

17. Department of Education (2014, Nov 27) Retrieved July 28, 2017 from https://www.gov.uk/government/news/guidance-on-promoting-british-values-in-schools-published. Contains public sector information licensed under the Open Government Licence v3.0.

18. Religious conservatism (2017, Jan 13) Retrieved Jan 11, 2017 from http://www.christianconcern.com/our-concerns/dame-louise-casey-religious-conservatism-is-often-anti-equalities

19. Faith minister's attack on Ashers (2016, Nov 23) Retrieved July 28, 2017 from http://www.christian.org.uk/news/faith-ministers-attack-ashers-touch.

20. Tatchell, P. (2016, Feb 1) I've changed my mind. The Guardian. Retrieved July 28, 2017 from https://www.theguardian.com/commentisfree/2016/feb/01/gay-cake-row-i-changed-my-mind-ashers-bakery-freedom-of-conscience-religion.

21. Christian Legal Centre Case Summaries 2006-2015. Retrieved July 28, 2017 from http://www.christianconcern.com/sites/default/files/clc_c

Chapter 4: Tactics of the Liberal Fascists

In chapter 2 we saw that there is a tolerance problem in Western society. Immigration, globalisation, technological development and secularisation have all led to a situation in which it is more difficult to talk meaningfully about finding shared values and therefore to agree on the boundaries of tolerance. In chapter 3 we sought to define liberal fascism and showed that while liberal fascists claim to be the champions of tolerance, this is in fact a myth. They believe in the superiority of their values and are intolerant of anyone who does not share them. Far from accepting behaviour and beliefs that are different from their own, they are seeking to force their own values on to others. So, what are some of the tactics that they are using to do this?

Political Correctness

The first tactic of the liberal fascists is what has become known as 'political correctness' (PC). It seems quite difficult to pin down exactly what PC is, but there are probably two features we need to consider: the underlying ideology and the practical outworking of those beliefs.

The key foundational principle of PC appears to be the belief that all human history is defined and determined by power relationships between different groups.

Generally speaking, white heterosexual men are considered to have dominated power structures in the Western world for many centuries and to have been responsible for oppressing just about everyone else! PC is a reaction against this perceived concentration and abuse of power and is therefore concerned with redistributing power from the powerful to the powerless:

> Automatically opposing the powerful and supporting the powerless means that when presented with a new issue, the politically correct must decide not what is right or wrong, malign or benign, true or untrue, but who is the more powerful and who the less powerful.[1]

All that is then required in any given situation is to identify the victim and support them, regardless of any other considerations. Anthony Browne suggests that PC should therefore be defined as:

> An ideology that classifies certain groups of people as victims in need of protection from criticism, and which makes believers feel that no dissent should be tolerated.[2]

In practice, opposing the powerful and supporting the powerless means avoiding anything that insults, offends or marginalises groups which are considered to fall into the 'powerless' category. It also means positively promoting, empowering and encouraging tolerance towards victimised groups and suppressing any alternative viewpoints. We could look at numerous examples of PC, particularly in areas such as human sexuality, gender politics, race, abortion, equality and diversity policies, and environmental issues, but three examples will suffice.

The first is the abuse of mainly white girls by largely Asian gangs in Rotherham in the late 1990's and early 2000's, which came to public attention in 2010. The case is complicated and many factors appear to have contributed to the abuse and the fact that it wasn't dealt with sooner; but one issue that was raised was that there was a misplaced sense of PC among the authorities which led to reluctance to tackle the problem. During two enquiries into the abuse scandal led by Professor Alexis Jay and then Louise Casey, it emerged that, because most of the perpetrators were of Pakistani heritage, council staff, police officers and others were nervous about identifying the ethnic origins of perpetrators for fear of being accused of racism. In her report Louise Casey concluded that:

> Rotherham's suppression of these uncomfortable issues and its fear of being branded racist has done a disservice to the Pakistani heritage community as well as the wider community. It has prevented discussion and effective action to tackle the problem. This has allowed perpetrators to remain at large, has let victims down, and perversely, has allowed the far right to try and exploit the situation. These may have been

unintended consequences but the impact remains the same and reaches into the present day...

A police officer was quoted as saying: "People were afraid that they'd get into trouble if they said something that was perceived as racist.... that was probably why the issue had been allowed to escalate so far, and that if someone had had the guts to stand up and say, 'I don't care what colour you are, that's a child', then maybe they could have dealt with it."[3]

Here we see the perversity of PC at work. We can only speculate about the motivation of those seeking to downplay the ethnic aspect of the abuse. Perhaps it was that they were wedded to an idea of multiculturalism that required them to avoid anything that might suggest failings within a particular community, or maybe it was driven by fear that by being honest about the abuse, relations between different communities would be damaged and intolerance would increase. Perhaps it was unacceptable to point the finger at members of an immigrant community that were considered to be one of the less powerful groups in society. Whatever the motivation, the outcome appears clear. Those who challenged the PC orthodoxy were considered insensitive and clearly worried that they might be seen as racist. Highlighting the fact that this abuse was the work of largely Asian gangs and that white girls were the main victims challenged underlying socio-political assumptions. People were not allowed to tell the truth or to speak their mind but had to conform to a liberal point of view concerned with promoting tolerance and avoiding offence, even if that meant turning a blind eye to the abuse of young people.

The Rotherham case is not simply one of historical interest. On the 9th of August 2017, eighteen people were convicted for being part of a network that sexually abused girls in Newcastle-Upon-Tyne. All but one of the perpetrators were Asian men and the victims were mainly white girls. Commenting on the case, Rotherham's Labour MP, Sarah Champion, expressed concern that society was still unwilling to face up to the fact that the perpetrators of this particular form of child abuse were predominantly Asian men from the British Pakistani community and added that "more people are afraid to be called a racist than they are afraid to be wrong about calling out child abuse."[4] She was subsequently forced to resign following complaints about an article she wrote in The Sun newspaper, which highlighted the issue of British Pakistani men abusing white girls. A number of Labour MPs accused The Sun of encouraging Islamophobia and it seems that her article was included in this criticism.[5] As a society we still appear to be unable to have a grown-up conversation about issues to do with race, without people being accused of racism or Islamophobia.

The second example of PC is one we have already touched on in chapter 3, where we referred to the way in which concern over immigration to the UK was often equated with racism and that debate around the issue was stifled as a result. This particularly came to light during the EU referendum campaign in 2016. On the first day of the campaign the Work and Pensions minister Priti Patel, who wanted Britain to leave the European Union, tackled this head on when she said in an interview with the Daily Telegraph that it was wrong to accuse people of racism just because they raised concerns about mass immigration.[6] She went on to criticise other politicians for creating a climate in which it was impossible to raise concerns about the impact of immigration without being accused of being racist. Once again PC was being used to impose a particular viewpoint upon society: 'immigration is good and if you don't agree you are probably racist'. The stigma of being accused of racism was enough to stop many people from voicing their genuine concerns.

A third example of PC is that of 'microaggressions'. These are classified as the casual, every day, often unintentional remarks or actions that send derogatory or negative messages to another person. The term was first used in the 1970's to describe the experience of black Americans and has subsequently been applied more widely to other marginalised groups. Those 'guilty' of microaggression usually belong to the dominant culture and the 'victim' is normally the member of a minority or marginalised group. An example would be to say, "I believe that the most qualified person should get the job." This could be considered a microaggression because it sends out the message that members of minority groups get an unfair advantage due to their race, colour, sexual orientation or disability etc. Asking someone where they are from could also be a microaggression if they are a member of a minority group, because it sends the message they are not really American/British/French, etc.

An example of the impact of this concept, was the banning of a Christian Union (CU) from a fresher's fair at an Oxford University College in October 2017. Balliol's Junior Common Room (JCR) committee banned the CU on the basis that its presence might make some students feel alienated, uncomfortable or unwelcome, due to the historic use of Christianity as an excuse for homophobia and neo-colonislaism.[7] As such its involvement could be considered as a microaggression.

Thoughtless actions and words can make others feel uncomfortable, so the concept of microaggression is not without merit, however in the final analysis it is a rather blatant attempt by liberals to impose their own worldview on others and to control the way people think and speak. It is also counterproductive in that it discourages people from interacting honestly with each other by creating a climate of fear, mistrust and victim-hood. It makes it more likely that people will retreat into ghettos where they only interact with those who think the same, rather than have open, genuine and honest conversations with others who may think differently. In the case of the CU that was banned from the fresher's fair, this action denied new students the opportunity to find out about the Christian faith, to have their preconceptions challenged and to understand more about the beliefs of others who have a different worldview. It also denied that opportunity to the CU members!

These brief examples illustrate the way in which PC is being used by the liberal fascists to impose their own beliefs and values on others and silence alternative viewpoints. While PC may have initially been beneficial to society in addressing issues of inequality and discrimination towards certain groups, its effects are now largely negative: it offends, closes-down freedom of expression, suppresses honest debate, creates a victim mentality among various groups, divides society, promotes intolerance towards those who do not agree with the liberal consensus and makes it more difficult for society to rationally identify and solve the problems that it faces.

The use of language – phobias and the rest

Very closely linked to political correctness is the use of language, in particular the proliferation of 'phobias'. A phobia is an extreme or irrational fear of something, but in common usage today it has a wider meaning of hatred towards a group of people; Islamophobia, homophobia and transphobia are perhaps the most common uses of the word in this context. As well as the word 'bigot', to which we have already referred, there are others such as racist, misogynist, or 'climate change denier' that are commonly used to label people who may not agree with the current liberal socio-political orthodoxy.

The point of these labels (or maybe we should say insults) is essentially to silence any opposition to liberal values by demonising those concerned. It's rather like the sketch in the Monty Python film, The Holy Grail, where a woman is accused of being a witch. She has clearly been dressed up by the villagers to look the part, but having been accused by them she is presumed guilty and no one is really interested in the evidence. In the same way, once someone has been accused of transgressing against the liberal orthodoxy and given the appropriate label, they are presumed guilty, whatever the pros and cons of the evidence concerned. As a guilty person, their views are suspect and not worth listening to. By accusing someone of a phobia there is no need to debate the issues, the argument is already won.

Another example is the use of the word 'populist'. Populism is the belief that power too often resides in the hands of small elites, political insiders and the wealthy. The role of populist movements is to challenge these vested interests and give power back to the 'ordinary people'. While populist movements can be of the political left, right or centre and the word can be used generally to describe ideas or policies whose only real virtue is their popularity, its main current usage is with reference to policies or parties who are considered illiberal and right wing. Political parties like the United

Kingdom Independence Party (UKIP), the National Front (NF) in France, Alternative for Deutschland (AfD) in Germany and politicians like Donald Trump in the US are all branded as populist. Needless to say, this is not a compliment but a thinly disguised term of abuse. If you are labelled as populist, then you really don't deserve to be listened to or taken seriously and are probably not very nice either (of course the idea that those on the left are somehow more virtuous and 'nice' is a fantasy that is soon dispelled by the facts of history in Stalin's Russia, Mao's China and Pol Pot's Cambodia). This is another example of the way in which language is being used to caricature, stigmatise, marginalise and silence those who do not fit in with the liberal orthodoxy. Dr Bruce Newsome of the University of California, Berkeley, comments that:

> Most uses of the term 'populism' seem to be motivated by left-wing denial of substantive opposition to the left-wing or 'liberal consensus.' The emerging problem with the 'liberal consensus' has been the conceit that it commands the truth.[8]

In other words, the liberal left seeks to recategorise popular views that fall outside of the liberal consensus as 'fringe right-wing populism', rather than admit that they are in fact a popular reaction against the arrogance of the liberal consensus. Labelling an individual or movement as 'populist' means that you do not need to engage with the underlying issues and face the possibility that the shortcomings of your own values and beliefs will be exposed. Demonising the opposition is far easier.

These examples of the use of language again demonstrate something of the mind-set of the liberal fascists. They are certain of the superiority of their own values, have closed minds that cannot see the weaknesses of their own belief system and are unable to conceive that they might learn something valuable from an alternative perspective. The old rhyme 'sticks and stones will break my bones, but names will never hurt me' is wide of the mark. The liberal fascists are successfully using language as a tool of intolerance, to close-down debate and marginalise those who have a different worldview.

Equality and Diversity

It is perhaps worth mentioning at this point the role played by 'equality and diversity' policies within public and private organisations:

> Equality and diversity is a term used in the United Kingdom to define and champion equality, diversity and human rights as defining values of society. It promotes equality of opportunity for all, giving every individual the chance to achieve their potential, free from prejudice and discrimination. UK legislation requires public authorities to promote equality in everything that they do, also making sure that other organisations meet their

legal duties to promote equality while also doing so themselves. In the UK under the Equality Act 2010 there are certain legal requirements under existing legislation to promote equality in the areas of nine protected characteristics.[9]

The protected characteristics are: sex, gender reassignment, disability, sexual orientation, religion or belief, race, age, pregnancy/maternity and marriage/civil partnership (in employment only). Those who have these characteristics are considered to be at higher risk of marginalisation or discrimination and hence need 'extra protection'.

This sounds great until we start to examine the way that equality and diversity policies are being applied within many organisations. Rather than celebrating and protecting diversity, it seems that too often they are being used to enforce conformity and coerce individuals into accepting certain values. So, in the case of Gary McFarlane (mentioned in the previous chapter), the reason for his dismissal was that he had breached his employer's equality and diversity policy by not wanting to be involved in providing sex therapy to same-sex couples; presumably this was seen as discriminating against them. However, the reason for his objection was his Christian faith, which you would have thought was both a protected characteristic and a reason for celebrating diversity! Instead, equality and diversity policies were used as a way of silencing and marginalising an individual who was not signed up to the liberal orthodoxy. Gary McFarlane was discriminated against for having values outside of the liberal consensus, even though the liberal consensus pretends to protect everybody from discrimination. He was treated unequally in the name of equality and was considered to be acting against diversity, though his very presence and behaviour was an expression of it.

No platforming

No platforming is a policy of the National Union of Students (NUS) of the United Kingdom.[10] Essentially its purpose is to prevent certain proscribed organisations or individuals whose views are perceived as offensive or harmful, from being given a platform to speak and it also bars union officers from sharing a platform with them. The proscribed organisations are mainly entities that the NUS consider to be racist or fascist. However, individual unions and associated campaigns can apply the policy to other organisations and individuals of their choosing. This policy is linked to the idea of 'safe spaces', which are places or environments in which an individual or group of people can feel confident that they will not be subjected to discrimination, criticism, harassment or harm. The term originated in educational establishments and was concerned with creating safe environments for those who felt marginalised, such as black or LGBT students.[11]

We have already mentioned an example of this policy in chapter 1, where students attempted to prevent

Germaine Greer speaking at the University of Cardiff, due to her 'controversial' views on transgender issues. Another example of this occurred in December 2015 when the Islamic Society at Goldsmiths College, London, sought to prevent Iranian born Maryam Namazie from giving a talk to the college's Atheist, Secularist and Humanist Society (Ash). Namazie, a spokesperson for the Council of Ex Muslims, was due to speak on the subject of blasphemy and apostasy in the age of Isis (Islamic State). The Islamic Society claimed that the talk, if given, would violate their right to a safe space. When the Student Union failed to prevent the talk going ahead, the Islamic Society disrupted the event and sought to intimidate those taking part in it. Both Goldsmith's LGBTQ and Feminist Societies offered their support to the Islamic Society and claimed that Maryam Namazie was an Islamophobe and that her presence was creating a climate of hatred.[12] Here is a very clear example of how the idea of safe spaces is used to close-down valid debate, in this case about certain aspects of Islam. It is also worth noting the irony of a situation in which an LGBTQ and Feminist group backed an Islamic society against secular humanists. It seems that political correctness has the effect of promoting hypocrisy as well as reducing the ability to think rationally. What mattered was not the values of the Islamic society, which would probably be unsympathetic to the LGBT and feminist cause, but rather their status as a 'victimised group'.

In another incident in 2010, two NUS officers at the University of Durham forced a proposed debate on multiculturalism to be cancelled. The debate was organised by Durham Union Society and was to have featured two prominent British National Party members: Andrew Brons MEP and Leeds City Councillor Chris Beverley. Upon hearing of BNP involvement in the debate, the two NUS officers demanded the debate's cancellation and threatened disruption if it wasn't. The subsequent cancellation of the event was met with a fierce backlash.[13] The no platforming policy was used to close-down debate and in this case demonstrated the intolerance of the NUS officers concerned towards anyone who did not agree with their take on multiculturalism.

While we may have some sympathy with the motivation behind these policies, the result is essentially to promote intolerance of viewpoints that differ from those held by the NUS. No platforming and safe spaces are forms of censorship by another name and fall into a familiar pattern of liberal fascists seeking to impose their values on to others and shut down the expression of alternative viewpoints. The issue of free speech on university campuses is one that has become increasingly high profile in the last few years. The online magazine Spiked has published an 'Annual Free Speech University Ranking' for British universities since 2015,[14] the results of which have been reported in major newspapers including the Guardian, Times and Daily Telegraph. Spiked claims that the results show increasing levels of censorship, driven as much by the university authorities as by student unions. The government has been concerned enough by this issue to set out plans to challenge the prevailing culture. The universities minister has indicated that part of the role of the newly created Office for Students (OfS) will be to ensure that universities protect freedom of speech and ensure that no platforming and safe spaces are not allowed to shut down healthy vigorous debate and the expression of alternative viewpoints.[15]

Universities and colleges should be places of learning, not indoctrination. Rather than restricting free speech, closing down debate and 'protecting' students from viewpoints that are deemed offensive or controversial, universities ought to provide an environment in which students' assumptions are challenged, where new ideas can be explored, debated, analysed and then accepted or refuted on the basis of evidence. While most people would probably agree that speech intended to stir up violence and hatred should be restricted, the examples we have looked do not fall into this category. The belief that surgery cannot make a man into a woman is a statement of fundamental belief about gender identity, rather than an attack on transgender people. Criticism of aspects of Islam (or any other belief system) is a legitimate activity in a liberal Western democracy and should not be viewed as evidence of Isalmophobia. In the same way, questioning the ideology and impact of multiculturalism does not make somcone a racist. Free speech may not be a 'blank cheque' in that most people would recognise the need for certain restrictions, but the liberal fascists seem rather too keen to close it down.

The instruments of the state

As secular liberalism has become the dominant worldview in the West and those who are liberal have taken over the reins of power, it is not surprising that they have sought to use that power to impose their beliefs on the rest of society. To this end every instrument of the state is being used: from the parliaments and legislative bodies at the top, through to the agencies of the state that run public services, the legal systems and courts that apply the laws, the education system that 'indoctrinates' the next generation in liberal values, the state funded media that gets the message out and even the charities and voluntary organisations that draw on public funding and therefore must accept the liberal orthodoxy.

We have already noted some ways in which the UK authorities have sought to impose their liberal values on to the rest of society. The Rotherham abuse case demonstrated the way in which political correctness had become ingrained in public bodies such as local government and the police. The liberal multicultural perspective was so sacrosanct that no one dared question it and if they did, they were silenced. We saw how the political class shut down debate on immigration by creating a climate in which those who questioned immigration levels were labelled as racist. The Asher's

Bakery case revealed how the legal system was being used to create a hierarchy of rights, namely the supremacy of 'equality' over freedom of speech, conscience and religion. We also saw that while the government's definition of British values included mutual respect and tolerance of those with different faiths and beliefs, this appeared to mean little if the views expressed clashed with the liberal orthodoxy.

There are many more examples we could give of the way in which liberal fascists use the power of the state to impose their values on others and silence those who hold different views. In 2012 a Brighton councillor was expelled from the Green Party for her opposition to same-sex marriage, based on her Christian convictions:

> Christina Summers, an elected Member of Brighton and Hove City Council, was dismissed from the Green Group of councillors for expressing her views on same-sex 'marriage' in a free vote. Councillors called for Christina to be dismissed after she voted against a motion at a Full Council meeting in support of the Government's plans to introduce same-sex 'marriage'. She explained that her decision was based on her Christian convictions, stating "I'm accountable to God above any political party." Commenting on Christina's vote, Deputy Council Leader, Phelim MacCafferty, the party spokesman on LGBT issues, said: "Greens believe she [Christina] is entitled to hold her view but this does not reflect the position,

spirit and track record of the Green Party in extending human and civil rights for all social groups irrespective of sexual orientation or on other grounds." Christina was dismissed from the Green Group of councillors for "bringing the party into disrepute." [16]

This example should need little comment as the implications are obvious. For all the warm words about tolerance, diversity, human rights and equality, the Green Party isn't tolerant and diverse enough to have within its ranks people who have a traditional view of human sexuality. Views that run counter to the liberal orthodoxy are to be silenced. Tolerance that extends only to views you agree with isn't tolerance at all.

In 2015, Richard Page, a Christian magistrate, was disciplined by a Cabinet minister and England's highest judge for saying that a child's best interests lie in being raised by a mother and a father. Richard, who had served as a magistrate in Kent for 15 years and was a well-respected member of the family court, expressed the view during a closed-door consultation with colleagues in a routine adoption case. Having heard all the evidence, Richard decided that his legal duty to act in the best interests of the child meant that he could not agree with placing the child with a same-sex couple. Following an investigation by the local Justice of the Peace Advisory Panel, the case was referred to the Lord Chancellor and the Lord Chief Justice. They gave Richard a public rebuke, saying that his Christian views about family life were discriminatory against same-sex couples and incompatible with his duties as a magistrate. He was barred from sitting in court until he completed 'equality training.' Richard said:

> "My Christian faith informs me that children flourish best in a loving home with a married mum and dad. My 20 years of experience in mental health service also leads me to the same conclusion. This is not a matter of prejudice or bigotry but is based on knowledge and evidence that I have applied when seeking the best interests for a lifetime of a vulnerable child."[17]

Once again, this example demonstrates the way in which the power of the state is being used to silence those who do not conform to the liberal orthodoxy and again the liberals' claim to be tolerant is shown to be a sham. In this instance, the Christian viewpoint was considered discriminatory against same sex couples; never mind that the views of the Lord Chief Justice discriminated against Christians and others who didn't share these liberal values. There is after all a hierarchy of rights and it appears that for some arbitrary reason, faith sits at the bottom of the pile.

In Scotland, the SNP (Scottish National Party), which considers itself a bastion of modernity and progressiveness, intended to bring into law in August 2016 a scheme whereby every child had a named state guardian to look after their welfare. Supporters claimed it was about avoiding another child abuse tragedy, whilst opponents said it was a snoopers' charter that would essentially allow the government to interfere in trivial aspects of children's lives and usurp the role of parents:

> On 28 July 2016, in the case of *The Christian Institute and others v The Lord Advocate (Scotland)* five UK Supreme Court judges unanimously struck down the central provisions of the scheme. The legislation required the named person to record and share confidential information concerning the wellbeing of children and their parents. The Court stated that these data sharing provisions in the Children and Young People (Scotland) Act breach the right to a private and family life under article 8 of the European Convention on Human Rights.[18]

In a line from the judgment, the Supreme Court Justices said:

> "The first thing that a totalitarian regime tries to do is to get at the children, to distance them from the subversive, varied influences of their families, and indoctrinate them in their rulers' view of the world." [19]

The judgement implied that there was at the very least a danger that the Scottish government would use the scheme to impose its values on to the nation's children, bypassing their parents if necessary.

Another example which is worth mentioning briefly concerned some advertising on buses in London. This case is noteworthy in that it very clearly demonstrates the way in which the power of the state is being used to promote liberal values, while suppressing alternative viewpoints. In 2012, the gay rights organisation Stonewall ran some adverts on the side of London buses which said 'Some people are Gay. Get over it!' This was part of the campaign for promoting gay marriage. Two Christian organisations wanted to run an advert that put an alternative viewpoint: 'Not Gay! Ex-Gay, Post-Gay and Proud. Get Over It!' Boris Johnson, the then Mayor of London, banned the advert stating that:

> "London is one of the most tolerant cities in the world and intolerant of intolerance. It is clearly offensive to suggest that being gay is an illness that someone recovers from and I am not prepared to have that suggestion driven around London on our buses."[20]

The Mayor's comments clearly demonstrated his own prejudice and intolerance of anyone who held a view of human sexuality that did not conform to the liberal orthodoxy. He might just as well have said, "London is one of the most tolerant cities in the world, as long as you agree with the views of its government."

The organisations involved in placing the advert were seeking to challenge the unproven assertion that people are 'born gay' and to stand up for the rights of people who wished to be helped with unwanted same-sex attraction. An examination of the literature on same-sex attraction reveals that its origins are varied, complex and poorly understood. Genetics, variations in the brain, as well as social, environmental and developmental factors may all play a part.[21] To claim that same-sex attraction is simply something a person is 'born with', which cannot or should not be changed is therefore over-simplistic, unsupported by the evidence and ideologically driven. As such it is wholly appropriate that the orthodox view should be challenged and that the needs and rights of those with unwanted same-sex attraction should be recognised. However, the idea that a gay person might not enthusiastically embrace their sexual orientation goes against the liberal orthodoxy and as such cannot be tolerated.

In some respects, it could be argued that the examples above simply reflect the outworking of democracy. Those who triumph at the ballot box have the power to implement their policies, which are then enforced by the instruments of the state. However, it isn't quite that simple. Democracy - at least in the way it is implemented in the West - is supposed to be about the will of the people being expressed through their elected representatives. The problem is that those who get voted into power frequently fail to secure the backing of even the majority of the people. In 2017 Donald Trump was elected by the American system of Electoral Colleges but did not win the national vote, which is something we heard a lot about from the liberal left who didn't like the result. In Tony Blair's election landslide in the UK in 1997, Labour got just over 43% of the vote, yet had a massive majority in Parliament. The deficiencies of the first past the post system in the UK meant that in 2015 UKIP got one seat with 12.6% of the vote whilst the Scottish National Party had 56 seats with only 4.7% of the vote. In the UK general election in 2010 the coalition government of Conservative and Liberal Democrats could claim that they had the majority of the votes cast, but that was on a voter turnout of 65.1%; so even they couldn't claim to represent the majority of citizens.

It is clear then that 'getting into government' doesn't usually equate to having the support of the majority of the people. As such, most democratically elected western governments do not have a 'mandate' to simply impose their will, values and beliefs on to wider society, without consideration of those who have an alternative viewpoint. To do so is just a form of 'elected dictatorship'. You might think that this knowledge would act as some sort of brake on political party's more contentious policies or that this would mean that politicians sought to build a consensus, but this does not appear to be the case. Whether liberal or conservative, right, left or centre, the temptation to use their power to the full is too great.

To reiterate, the issue for liberals is that they claim to be champions of tolerance, unlike those on the right who make no such assertion. Tolerance is a willingness to accept that others behave or think differently than you do; but, more than that, it involves not seeking to force your own beliefs and values on to other people. As the examples above have shown, while claiming to believe in and champion tolerance, the liberal fascists are using the state to impose their values on society in a way that is often intolerant of others who have a different opinion. As such, Donald Trump is no different than Hillary Clinton and the United Kingdom Independence Party - if it ever got into power - would be no different than the Labour or Conservative Party. Liberal fascists don't really believe in tolerance any more than those they accuse of intolerance. Both seek to use power to impose their values on others, often with little regard to the problems this will cause or to the possibility that the 'other side' might have something useful to say.

The Power of Celebrity

It's not exactly a revelation to say that Western culture is obsessed with celebrity. Hello Magazine, Celebrity MasterChef, I'm a Celebrity Get Me Out of Here, Celebrity Big Brother, endless newspaper columns, and a plethora of award ceremonies including the Oscars and BAFTAs, are all testimony to the cult of celebrity. Some are celebrities because of their achievements and others are famous just for being famous. Whatever the reason for their celebrity status, the received wisdom seems to be that your cause will be helped by wheeling out some celebrities to show their support for it. After all they are famous, popular, good-looking, likeable and trendy, so if they support your cause it must be good, maybe even right! Quite why being a famous actor/actress, author, sports personality or musician, gives an individual special insight into the complex problems of humanity and makes them worth listening to is unclear, but apparently it does.

The liberals have been particularly adept at harnessing the power of celebrity for their cause and given that the arts are generally an area in which liberal values thrive, this probably isn't surprising. Anyone who lived through it will remember the visit on Wednesday 30th July 1997 of Noel Gallagher, Meg Mathews, Lenny Henry, Simon Mayo, Anita Roddick and Tony "Baldrick" Robinson, among others, to Downing Street to congratulate the new Prime Minister Tony Blair on his victory. If you voted for Tony you were definitely on the side of coolness and modernity and therefore probably right as well. Unfortunately, the love affair between celebrity and New Labour didn't last that long.

In April 2016 Bruce Springsteen and his E Street Band cancelled a concert scheduled in North Carolina, in protest at the State's so-called 'bathroom law' which barred transgender individuals from using public bathrooms and locker rooms that didn't correspond with their gender at birth.[22] Springsteen described his actions as a fight against prejudice and bigotry and being a celebrity, he got lots of publicity and praise. Of course, another way of looking at it is that he just demonstrated his own prejudice and intolerance of those who held an alternative viewpoint; after all, those who backed the law have valid concerns. Women have every right to feel uncomfortable about the possibility of sharing changing and showering facilities with people with penises and given the lengths that paedophiles go to in order to gain access to children, people have good reason to be concerned about 'anatomical males' using the same facilities as girls. Additionally, it is right to ask why the needs of a very small number of transgender people should take priority over those of other larger minorities (e.g. women) and be viewed as more important than ensuring the safety of children and young people. It is not that the rights and needs of transgender people are unimportant, rather that they should to be balanced against those of the rest of society.

In the 2016 US elections the Democrats really pulled out the stops, lining up celebrities to say how nice Hillary was, at least compared to the other guy. Meryl Streep, Samuel L. Jackson, J.K. Rowling, George Clooney and Madonna, to name but a few, all spoke out against the election of Donald Trump. Their views were widely reported, as if their celebrity status somehow gave them not only special insight, but also the right to be heard.

At this point you might be asking what the power of celebrity has got to do with tolerance. The link may seem tenuous, but there is a subtle way in which this plays into the whole idea that liberal values are self-evidently right and superior and therefore those who oppose them are to be dismissed as irrelevant. These successful, beautiful people embrace liberal values, so you should too. If you don't then why should you be listened to? There is probably something wrong with you!

The media

If you want to get your message out, then you have to use the media to do it. While the media in the Western world is a mixed bag of left and right, conservative and liberal, it is certainly used as a tool by the liberal fascists to both promote their own values and to discredit those with whom they disagree. The tactics of the media in this respect include focusing on some stories while ignoring others, emphasising certain parts of a story whilst minimising others, choosing to interview certain individuals as a way of enhancing or discrediting particular viewpoints, the misuse of statistics and sometimes simply repeating or perpetuating falsehoods. One of the big stories at the moment is the idea of fake news, where hoaxes, propaganda and disinformation are put out as if they are real news. While the use of the internet and social media to do this may be a new phenomenon, this sort of thing has been going on ever since the media existed. A work colleague recently told me that he goes to at least four very different web sites for news and hopes that between them he might get some idea of the truth. You certainly won't get impartial news by going to any one media outlet and this is even true of the BBC.

The BBC has a particularly important part in the culture and life of the UK and while its editorial policy states that it should be impartial, it is no secret that it has a liberal cultural bias. Andrew Marr, who was the political editor of the BBC news commented that:

> "The BBC is not impartial or neutral. It's a publicly funded, urban organisation with an abnormally large number of young people, ethnic minorities, and gay people. It has a liberal bias, not so much a party-political bias. It is better expressed as a cultural liberal bias."[23]

Of course, the BBC has been accused of all kinds of bias over the years, but as someone who regularly uses its website and listens to Radio 4 news programmes at least once a day, I would say that Andrew Marr's comments 'hit the nail on the head'. It matters because many people don't feel they can trust the BBC any more to be an impartial bearer of news and comment. It has become a tool for the promotion of cultural liberalism.

Intimidation

Last, but not least, the liberal fascists are willing to use intimidation and violence to get their way, shut down debate and impose their values on others. The Nazis had the Brown-shirts, Mussolini had the Black-shirts, Mao had the Red Guards and the liberal fascists have a rag tag of various groups who are happy to turn out and intimidate their opponents and if necessary destroy property and resort to physical violence. In the UK, groups like Unite Against Fascism have been involved in violence against people they consider to be fascists,[24] often in full view of the TV cameras and recorded for posterity on YouTube. In the US, an anti-fascist grouping called Antifa has become increasingly violent following the election of Donald Trump. They are committed to the direct action and the use of violence against 'fascists'.[25] Along with anarchists and anti-globalization groups, these organisations form an unpleasant rent-a-mob that takes the intolerance of the liberal fascists on to the streets. You won't find mainstream liberal politicians condoning such actions, but neither will you hear strong condemnation. Furthermore, if you look into who is associated with organisations like Unite Against Fascism, you will find the names of mainstream Trade Unions and senior politicians crop up as founders, supporters, donors and board members. Even David Cameron, the Conservative Ex-Prime Minister, was a founding signatory.[26]

Both examples used in the section on 'no platforming' demonstrated the willingness of the liberal fascists to use or threaten intimidation and violence to shut down debate. A video of the harassment of Maryam Namazie at Goldsmiths College is available on YouTube[27] and makes unpleasant viewing as a group of Muslim students essentially intimidate her as she attempts to give her talk on blasphemy and apostasy. So much for tolerance. In the incident at Durham University where two BNP members were to speak at a debate on multiculturalism, the two NUS officers incorrectly stated that the debate would be illegal and threatened to organise a colossal demonstration in tandem with Unite Against Fascism, adding that, "If any students are hurt in and around this event responsibility will lie with you."[28] The threat of potential violence if the event continued was clear. More recently in November 2017, an event organised by the pro-life group, Oxford Students for Life to discuss the upcoming abortion referendum in Ireland, was disrupted by feminist students from the Oxford Student Union's 'Women's Campaign', who shouted the speaker down and prevented the event from going on for 40 minutes. They refused to leave when asked to by security guards and the police had to be called.[29] The feminist group made no attempt to engage in dialogue, but instead seemed intent on preventing others from exercising their right to free speech.

Similar patterns of behaviour are found in other Western countries. Legitimate protest at the election of Donald Trump turned into violence on the day of his inauguration. Trump supporters and the police were attacked and property damaged.[30] In February 2017, left-wing demonstrators attacked supporters of the French National Front party as they were making their way to a rally in Nantes.[31] In Germany, the congress of the anti-immigrant Alternative for Deutschland party held in April 2016 was attacked by left wing demonstrators and a number of police and AfD members were injured.[32] The obvious irony is that in all of these cases the protestors would no doubt claim to be demonstrating against intolerance and yet they are exhibiting the very same thing by their actions. They are 'anti-fascist fascists'!

The willingness of the liberal fascists to threaten or use violence and intimidation against those with different views once again demonstrates that their claim to be champions of tolerance is in fact a hollow deception. Intimidating or assaulting another person because they are seeking to express 'right-wing opinions', cannot in any way be dressed up as tolerant.

Intolerant champions of tolerance

The liberal fascists are utterly convinced of the superiority and truth of their own values and as such are intolerant of anybody who does not share them. They appear oblivious to the resulting inherent contradiction of claiming to be champions of tolerance, while being fundamentally intolerant! In this chapter we have seen how they are using political correctness, language, equality and diversity policies, no platforming, safe spaces, the instruments of the state, the media, the power of celebrity and intimidation and violence to impose their views on to wider society. Of course, the intolerance of the liberal fascists pales into insignificance when compared to the 'fascism' of the Nazis, Stalinists, Maoists, Khmer Rouge or Islamic State etc., but if it is not exposed and instead allowed to grow and flourish, who knows where it will eventually lead.

Currently, those who dissent from the liberal orthodoxy may 'only' lose their job, face disciplinary procedures or side-lining at work, suffer the scorn of those around them, find themselves dragged before the courts and be denied the right of freedom of belief and conscience etc.[33] However, it isn't a huge step to imagine a situation where such dissent is criminalised, with appropriate penalties. Those who hold traditional views about such things as marriage or human sexuality are already being branded extremist and accused of hatred, so it doesn't take a significant leap of the imagination to think that otherwise law-abiding citizens could soon find themselves cast as criminals, social pariahs or enemies of the state because they do not embrace so-called liberal values.

Following a number of terrorist attacks in the UK in 2017, the Prime Minister, Theresa May, spoke about the government's determination to tackle extremism and said that a new commission would be set up whose role would be to identify, expose and counter it.[34] While this may sound welcome, it raises questions about how extremism is defined. The concern is that any views that do not fit in with the liberal consensus will be branded as extremist and the fight against extremism will be used as an excuse to silence those whose values are socially conservative. If that is the case, we can say goodbye to any notion of a tolerant society.

References

1. Browne, A., The Retreat of Reason: Political correctness and the corruption of public debate in modern Britain (Civitas, 2006) page 11.

2. Browne, A., The Retreat of Reason: Political correctness and the corruption of public debate in modern Britain (Civitas, 2006) page 4.

3. Casey, L. (2015, Feb 04) Report of Inspection of Rotherham Metropolitan Borough Council. Retrieved July 29, 2017 from https://www.gov.uk/government/uploads/system/uploads/attachment_data/file/401125/46966_Report_of_Inspection_of_Rotherham_WEB.pdf, page 36. Contains public sector information licensed under the Open Government Licence v3.0.

4. Maidment, J. (2017, August 10) People care more about being called racist. The Telegraph. Retrieved September 12, 2017 from http://www.telegraph.co.uk/news/2017/08/10/fear-called-racist-stops-people-reporting-child-sexual-exploitation/

5. McCann, K. (2017, August 17) Sarah Champion used as a scapegoat. The Daily Telegraph. Retrieved August 19, 2017 from http://www.telegraph.co.uk/news/2017/08/17/sarah-champion-used-scapegoat-warning-cultural-link-child-sex/

6. Hope, C. (2016, April 16) Priti Patel interview. The Telegraph. Retrieved July 30, 2017 from http://www.telegraph.co.uk/news/2016/04/15/priti-patel-interview-its-not-racist-to-worry-about-immigration/.

7. Turner, C. (2017, Oct 10). Oxford college bans 'harmful' Christian Union. The Telegraph. Retrieved Oct 30, 2017 from http://www.telegraph.co.uk/education/2017/10/10/oxford-college-bans-harmful-christian-union-freshers-fair/

8. Newsome, B. (2016, Dec 11) Stop blaming 'populism' for everything. Retrieved July 20, 2017 from http://blogs.berkeley.edu/2016/12/11/populism-cant-be-blamed-for-everything.

9. Equality and diversity (United Kingdom). (2017, June 10). In *Wikipedia, The Free Encyclopaedia*. Retrieved 07:26, July 20, 2017, from https://en.wikipedia.org/w/index.php?title=Equality_and_diversity_(United_King dom)&oldid=784885371. Licenced under CC-BY-SA 3.0. https://creativecommons.org/licenses/by-sa/3.0/

10. No Platform. (2017, November 7). In *Wikipedia, The Free Encyclopaedia*. Retrieved 18:34, November 28, 2017, from https://en.wikipedia.org/w/index.php?title=No_Plat form&oldid=809213751. Licenced under CC-BY-SA 3.0. https://creativecommons.org/licenses/by-sa/3.0/

11. Safe-space. (2017, July 29). In *Wikipedia, The Free Encyclopaedia*. Retrieved 15:30, July 30, 2017, from https://en.wikipedia.org/w/index.php?title=Safe-space&oldid=792860494. Licenced under CC-BY-SA 3.0. https://creativecommons.org/licenses/by-sa/3.0/

12. Ali, A. (2015, December 4). Muslim Students. The Independent. Retrieved Nov 17, 2017 from http://www.independent.co.uk/student/news/muslim-students-from-goldsmiths-university-s-islamic-society-heckle-and-aggressively-interrupt-a6760306.html

13. Student Union to quit NUS (2010, March 19). The Durham Advertiser. Retrieved Nov 17, 2017 from http://www.durhamadvertiser.co.uk/news/5072271.display/

14. The Free Speech University Rankings. Retrieved Nov 28, 2017 fromhttp://www.spiked-online.com/free-speech-university-rankings.

15. Telegraph Reporters (2017, Oct 19). Free Speech. Daily Telegraph. Retrieved Nov 28, 2017 from http://www.telegraph.co.uk/news/2017/10/19/universities-told-must-commit-free-speech-new-plans/

16. Christian Legal Centre Case Summaries 2006-2015. Retrieved July 28, 2017 from http://www.christianconcern.com/sites/default/files/clc_case_summaries_v7.pdf. Licenced under CC BY-ND 2.0 UK. https://creativecommons.org/licenses/by-nd/2.0/uk/

17. Christian Legal Centre Case Summaries 2006-2015. Retrieved July 28, 2017 from http://www.christianconcern.com/sites/default/files/clc_c ase_summaries_v7.pdf. Licenced under CC BY-ND 2.0 UK. https://creativecommons.org/licenses/by-nd/2.0/uk/

18. Named Persons scheme judicial review. Retrieved July 30, 2017 from http://www.christian.org.uk/case/named-person-scheme/

19. Named Persons scheme unlawful. Retrieved July 30, 2017 from http://www.christianconcern.com/our-concerns/adoption/named-person-scheme-unlawful-rules-supreme-court. Licenced under CC BY-ND 2.0 UK. https://creativecommons.org/licenses/by-nd/2.0/uk/

20. Bingham, J. (2012, April 12) Boris Johnson bans 'gay cure' advert. The Telegraph. Retrieved August 6, 2017 from http://www.telegraph.co.uk/news/politics/9201095/Boris-Johnson-bans-gay-cure-bus-adverts.html.

21.Harrison, G. (2008) The science behind same sex attraction. Retrieved March 29, 2018 from http://www.cmf.org.uk/resources/publications/content/?c ontext=article&id=2078

22. Holpuch, A (2016, April 9) Anti-LGBT law. The Guardian. Retrieved Nov 17, 2017 from https://www.theguardian.com/music/2016/apr/08/bruce-springsteen-cancels-north-carolina-concert-lgbt-discrimination-law

23. Hannan, D. (2012, Aug 14) How we counter the BBC's liberal bias. The Telegraph. Retrieved July 30, 2017 from http://www.telegraph.co.uk/culture/tvandradio/bbc/9475479/Heres-how-we-counter-the-BBCs-liberal-bias.html.

24.Smith, L. (2010, March 22) Police blame anti-fascists. The Independent. Retrieved Nov 7, 2017 from http://www.independent.co.uk/news/uk/crime/police-blame-anti-fascists-for-violence-1925038.html

25. Antifa (United States). (2017, November 7). In *Wikipedia, The Free Encyclopedia*. Retrieved 14:31, November 7, 2017, from https://en.wikipedia.org/w/index.php?title=Antifa_(United_States)&oldid=809118108. Licenced under CC-BY-SA 3.0. https://creativecommons.org/licenses/by-sa/3.0/

26. Founding Signatories. Retrieved July 20, 2017 from http://uaf.org.uk/about/founding-signatories/.

27. Godless Spellchecker (2015, Dec 3) ISOC Islamist Thugs Attempt To Intimidate Maryam N. Retrieved July 20, 2017 from https://www.youtube.com/watch?v=kl0sI47t. VgY.

28. Student Union to quit NUS (2010, March 19). The Durham Advertiser. Retrieved Nov 17, 2017 from http://www.durhamadvertiser.co.uk/news/5072271.display/

29. Cummings-McLean, D. (2017, Nov 3) Oxford Students for Life. Retrieved Nov 7, 2017 from https://www.lifesitenews.com/news/police-remove-screaming-feminists-from-pro-life-meeting-at-uk-university

30. Vargas, T. (2017, Jan 20) Inauguration protesters. The Washington Post. Retrieved Nov 7, 2017 from https://www.washingtonpost.com/local/protesters-bring-shouts-skirmishes-and-shutdowns-to-inauguration-celebration/2017/01/20/00ea4c72-df11-11e6-acdf-14da832ae861_story.html?utm_term=.9d8886001348

31. Moore, F. (2017, March 1) Protesters launch attack. The Express. Retrieved Nov 7, 2017 from http://www.express.co.uk/news/world/772506/front-national-marine-le-pen-zenith-nantes-attack-protesters

32. Reuters (2016, April 30) Left-wing protesters. The Telegraph. Retrieved Nov 7.2017 from http://www.telegraph.co.uk/news/2016/04/30/left-wing-protesters-clash-with-german-police-before-right-wing/

33. Christian Legal Centre Case Summaries 2006-2015. Retrieved July 28, 2017 from http://www.christianconcern.com https://creativecommons.org/licenses/by-nd/2.0/uk//sites/default/files/clc_case_summaries_v7.pdf. Licenced under CC BY-ND 2.0 UK. https://creativecommons.org/licenses/by-nd/2.0/uk/.

34. Travis, T. (2017, May 25) Theresa May plans anti-extremism drive. The Guardian. Retrieved July 28, 2017 from https://www.theguardian.com/politics/2017/may/25/theresa-may-anti-extremism-drive-tories-manchester-attack.

Chapter 5: Multiculturalism

Before moving on to consider how Western society might be more authentically tolerant, we need to specifically address the issue of multiculturalism, which poses a significant challenge to the notion of tolerance in Western societies.

Multiculturalism is a term used in both sociology and political philosophy... it can mean a cultural pluralism in which the various ethnic groups collaborate and dialog with one another without having to sacrifice their particular identities. In sociology and everyday usage, it is a synonym for pluralism with the two terms often used interchangeably and refers to either specific mixed ethnic community areas where multiple cultural traditions exist or a single country within which they do... Multiculturalism as a political philosophy involves ideologies and policies which vary widely, ranging from the advocacy of equal respect to the various cultures in a society, to policies of promoting the maintenance of cultural diversity.[1]

Multiculturalism and the tolerance problem

As we recognised in chapter 2, the increasing diversity of Western society makes it more difficult to agree on the boundaries of tolerance. Immigrants have arrived from all over the world and brought with them their own cultures, religions and worldviews, the values of which are not always compatible with the norms of Western culture. Over time this has inevitably led to a 'culture clash' and in some instances to the outlawing of certain practices that are considered incompatible with Western values. The boundaries of tolerance have been reached.

For example, in some cultures arranged marriages are common and sometimes these can end up being forced, where at least one of the people concerned faces physical or psychological pressure to get married. This problem has been recognised in the UK and forced marriage is now illegal in England and Wales. The government has set up a unit to specifically deal with the issue. According to the Home Office, in 2016, the Forced Marriage Unit gave advice or support related to a possible forced marriage in 1,428 cases. In 43% of cases, the country the forced marriage risk related to was Pakistan, followed by Bangladesh at 8% and India at 6%.[2]

Another example is Female genital mutilation. This is

> A practice that is carried out for various cultural, religious and social reasons within families and communities, in the mistaken belief that it will benefit the girl in some way (for example, as a preparation for marriage or to preserve her virginity).[3]

It is found in communities from at least 16 countries across Africa, the Middle East and South-East Asia. According to The World Health Organisation approximately three million girls are affected annually. The practice has no health benefits for the child concerned but can lead to both physical and mental harm. As a result, the practice has been outlawed in the UK.

Then there is the issue of honour crimes. These attacks are punishments on people, usually women, for acts that are considered to have brought shame on their family. Such attacks can include acid attacks, abduction, mutilations, beatings and in some cases, murder. The reasons for the victims bringing shame on the family can vary, but include:

> Refusing to enter an arranged marriage, being in a relationship that is disapproved by their family, having sex outside marriage, becoming the victim of rape, dressing in ways which are deemed inappropriate, engaging in non-heterosexual relations or renouncing a faith.[4]

Although these occur throughout the world, they are particularly prevalent within the Middle East and South Asia and are therefore associated with immigrant communities in the West which originate from these areas. There have been a number of well publicised cases in the UK, including that of Shafilea Iftikhar Ahmed, a 17-year-old British Pakistani girl from Great Sankey, Warrington, Cheshire, who was murdered by her parents in 2003 for refusing an arranged marriage. The parents saw this as bringing shame upon their family. Over 11,000 cases of honour crimes were recorded by the police in the UK between 2010 and 2014.[5] Obviously these practices are illegal in the UK, but the reason for mentioning them is that they demonstrate how large a gap exists between the beliefs and values of wider Western culture and some of those who have more recently settled here.

While some cultural practices have been identified as so out of step with Western values that they have been outlawed, others remain legal but still raise questions around the boundaries of tolerance. One such issue that is under scrutiny in the UK is that of Sharia courts or councils. These are bodies which provide legal rulings and advice to Muslims, based on the interpretation of Islamic Sharia law. They have no formal legal authority and those using them would have to accept their rulings voluntarily. In 2016 the UK government launched a review into the way these courts work, amid concerns that:

> There is evidence some sharia councils may be working in a discriminatory and unacceptable way, seeking to legitimise forced marriage and issuing divorces that are unfair to women, contrary to the teachings of Islam.[6]

Theresa May, the Home Secretary at the time said:

"A number of women have reportedly been victims of what appear to be discriminatory decisions taken by sharia councils, and that is a significant concern. There is only one rule of law in our country, which provides rights and security for every citizen." [7]

The intention of the government appears to be to make sure that these courts are operating in accordance with UK law. The concern is that they reflect cultural values which essentially discriminate against women.

Another issue where there is a clear clash of cultures is that of freedom of speech, particularly with reference to religion. In Western societies, religion is now considered a legitimate area for debate, discussion and even ridicule. Christians have long accepted that one of the costs of freedom of religion in a secular society is the freedom of others to both criticise and mock their beliefs. However, some of those coming from other cultures have very different attitudes and do not accept such behaviour. The production of images of Mohammed is a case in point. On a number of occasions when images of Mohammed have been published in Western magazines or newspapers, there has been a violent response from some within the Muslim community. The worst case of this occurred in 2015 when ten journalists and two policemen were killed at the Charlie Hebdo magazine office in Paris, after the magazine had printed cartoons depicting Mohammed. Clearly these images were offensive to Muslims, but what the incident demonstrated was the gulf in values between some Muslims in Europe and wider Western society. The Charlie Hebdo magazine has been equally offensive to other groups, including Catholics, but in these cases the 'victims' hadn't responded by seeking to murder the magazine's staff! Remember the words of Evelyn Beatrice Hall (often misattributed to the French Philosopher Voltaire); "I disapprove of what you say, but I will defend to the death your right to say it." [8] Freedom of speech cannot exist in any meaningful sense, without the assumption that it is okay to express opinions that others may find objectionable.

A further example is the freedom of people to choose their religion or non-religion. This is something we take for granted in Western society but is not necessarily a value that is shared by some within immigrant communities. This is a particular issue within Islam, where apostasy (leaving the faith) is often seen as a grave crime. Sixteen Muslim countries criminalise public apostasy and in at least eight of these, it is punishable by death.[9] As a result, some Muslims who want to leave Islam, can face hostility and persecution. In response to the ill treatment experienced by some in the UK who have left Islam and become Christians, the organisation Christian Concern has launched an initiative called 'Safe Haven' to offer protection, advice and support and to establish a network of safe houses where ex-Muslims can find refuge.[10]

What these examples illustrate is the fact that multiculturalism raises additional problems around the notion of tolerance. How much should Western society tolerate the values and beliefs of other cultures, particularly if they clash with generally accepted Western values? What are the boundaries? As the size of immigrant communities grows in Western countries, the question becomes even more significant. Is there a point at which Western values themselves are threatened or undermined by multiculturalism? Liberal Western democracy has always carried within itself the seeds of its own destruction in that the democratic process potentially provides illiberal and anti-democratic forces with the opportunity to come to power.

Cultural Relativism

At this point we ought to look briefly at the anthropological concept of cultural relativism. This answers the question about how we should interact with other cultures by saying that:

> A person's beliefs, values and practices should be understood based on that person's own culture, rather than judged against the criteria of another.[11]

In other words, right and wrong become 'local' and specific to an individual culture. There is no universal moral standard against which all cultures should be measured, so no society has the right to judge another's beliefs or customs. In the multicultural context this means that all cultures are treated with equal respect; therefore, it is inappropriate to talk about cultures being in any way inferior or superior to others and it is wrong for one culture to seek to impose its values on to another. As we have already seen in the previous chapter, this idea has found its way into wider society and is partly the reason why many in the West have been reluctant to criticise some of the beliefs and practices of immigrant communities that are at odds with Western values. To do so would be to suggest that Western culture is superior, which smacks too much of colonialism, imperialism, intolerance and even racism. Given that all of these 'isms' have at their root a sense of cultural superiority, the obvious antidote is relativism.

Cultural relativism may well have some positive attributes. As a methodological tool it can be helpful to anthropologists in their academic studies, as it enables them to suspend judgement and stay detached from the cultures they observe. It also challenges all of us to critically examine our own culture, rather than just assume that what we believe or the way we do things is always right or 'the best' (ethnocentrism). Those who live and work in other countries, often come to appreciate certain aspects of the 'local culture' and return 'home' feeling that their own society has something to learn.

However, cultural relativism also has some significant flaws. Firstly, it doesn't seem to match with human experience. When we see or experience evil, pain, suffering or injustice, most of us have an inbuilt gut reaction which tells us that something is wrong. When we hear of Islamic State selling off captured women as sex slaves or the Taliban (a Sunni Islamic political movement in Afghanistan) denying girls an education, we don't simply think of it as an interesting feature of their culture! While this reaction may partly be driven by cultural factors, there is surely something else going on. In his book *Mere Christianity*, the well-known Christian academic and author C. S. Lewis, puts this down to the fact that there is a 'law of nature' or 'decent behaviour' that is known to all people.[12] He suggests that anyone taking the trouble to study the moral teaching of ancient cultures will find that while there were differences in morality, these never amounted to anything like a total difference. For example, societies differed as to how many wives a man could have, but no society ever said a man could just take whatever woman he wanted. Equally, no society ever admired cowardice, or glorified those who ran away in battle! The belief that there is some sort of 'universal moral law' provides the foundation for the Universal Declaration of Human Rights, proclaimed by the United Nations General Assembly in Paris on 10 December 1948.[13] There would be no place for such a declaration in the world of 'cultural relativism'.

Secondly, while cultural relativism might work in a context where different cultures have very little to do with each other, it appears increasingly obvious that it cannot work in a multicultural context. As the ancient Greek historian Herodotus pointed out, human nature is such that most societies consider their own customs and beliefs as the norm and superior to those of others.[14] In the multicultural context this means that a certain amount of conflict is inevitable between different cultural groups. Social practices and beliefs which seem normal to one group may be considered alien, annoying, socially unacceptable, or even evil and immoral to another. Additionally, if we accept the notion of the existence of a universal moral law, it is inevitable that this will be used as a measure against which all cultures are judged and that this will lead to value judgements being made about the merits or otherwise of different cultural viewpoints and practices. For example, if we believe that men and women are fundamentally equal, we are likely to consider Western culture superior in this respect to the cultural vision of the Taliban.

Thirdly, as with other forms of relativism, the concept is internally inconsistent. Relativism denies that absolute truth exists, but in doing so makes a claim to absolute truth. Essentially it states that 'all truth is relative' apart from the absolute claim that 'all truth is relative'.

Changing attitudes to multiculturalism

As some of the potential problems of multiculturalism have become clearer, so the attitudes of Western governments and societies to it have begun to change. Initially multiculturalism embraced the idea of maintaining the identity of distinctive cultures and many Western governments officially adopted policies based on these ideas from the 1970's onwards but, due to growing unease about the segregation of communities and the radicalisation of young people who felt no attachment to wider society, many Western governments have started to talk more about integration and social cohesion. After the London bombings in July 2005, the then British Prime Minister Tony Blair said that:

"The right to be in a multicultural society was always implicitly balanced by a duty to integrate and be part of Britain, to be British and Asian, British and black, British and white... When it comes to our essential values, the belief in democracy, the rule of law, tolerance, equal treatment for all, respect for this country and its shared heritage — then that is where we come together, it is what gives us what we hold in common; it is what gives us the right to call ourselves British... At that point, no distinctive culture or religion supersedes our duty to be part of an integrated United Kingdom."[15]

In 2011 David Cameron speaking at a security conference in Munich echoed the same sentiments, when he said:

"Under the doctrine of state multiculturalism, we have encouraged different cultures to live separate lives, apart from each other and apart from the mainstream. We've failed to provide a vision of society to which they feel they want to belong. We've even tolerated these segregated communities behaving in ways that run completely counter to our values."[16]

The need to promote a set of common values around which people could unite and to prevent the segregation of communities, led the Conservative/Lib Dem coalition government to formalise and promote the idea of 'British values', to which we have already referred. It was no longer seen as acceptable for certain groups to live out and promote values that contradicted those of mainstream society. Being British had to mean accepting the core values of democracy, the rule of law, individual liberty and mutual respect and tolerance of those with different faiths and beliefs.

This 'change of heart' among mainstream politicians was also driven by a growing unease among sections of the electorate about levels of immigration and the effects of multiculturalism. Established political parties have had to rethink their approach to these issues as we have witnessed the growing power and influence of 'right wing' parties who, one suspects, reject the idea of multiculturalism completely. For example, in the German Federal Parliament elections in 2017, the anti-immigrant party, Alternative for Deutschland, became the third largest party in the Bundestag with 12.6% of the vote.[17] Similar political movements have had increasing influence in other European countries including France, the Netherlands, Austria and Italy.

Multiculturalism and the contradictions of liberal thinking

Given the obvious differences between the socially conservative values of many immigrant communities and the values of those on the liberal left, you might have thought that liberals would have mixed feelings about multiculturalism, but nothing could be further from the truth. This had led to the situation where those on the liberal left have frequently championed causes and groups whose values are significantly at odds with their own.

In chapter 3 we mentioned the case of Maryam Namazie who in December 2015 came to Goldsmiths College London to give a talk to the college's Atheist, Secularist and Humanist Society (Ash) on the subject of blasphemy and apostasy in the age of Isis. The Islamic Society claimed that the talk, if given, would violate their right to a safe space. When the Student Union failed to prevent the talk going ahead the Islamic Society disrupted the event and sought to intimidate those taking part in it. Both Goldsmith's LGBTQ and Feminist societies offered their support to the Islamic Society and claimed that Maryam Namazie was an Islamophobe and that her presence was creating a climate of hatred. This illustrates the crazy mixed up thinking of the liberal left. The values of the Atheist,

Secularist and Humanist Society, would have no doubt been far closer to the LGBTQ and Feminist Societies, but these groups chose to offer their support to the Islamic Society instead, who if faithful to the orthodox teachings of Islam, would reject the basic notions of feminism and LGBTQ rights. There are at least eight countries around the world where homosexual acts can be punished by death and all but one is majority Muslim.[18] The reaction to Maryam Namazine fits a pattern which we have highlighted on a number of occasions. Any criticism of Islam or the behaviour of some within Muslim communities, however justified, is automatically branded as Islamophobia.

Another example, this time from the Netherlands, is that of Ayaan Hirsi Ali, a feminist and writer, who was born in Somalia and obtained political asylum in the Netherlands in 1992. She came into the spotlight in 2001 for speaking publicly about what she saw as the repression of Muslim women in the Netherlands and the failure of the Dutch political Left to deal with the problem. She believed that the reason for this failure was the policy of multiculturalism, which she considered to be responsible for giving respectability to cultures that oppressed women.[19] In her view the paradox was that on one hand the Dutch political left supported ideas of equality and emancipation for women, but in the case of Muslim women, they did nothing about it and even facilitated their oppression through the policies of multiculturalism. Since her open criticism of Islam in 2002, she has lived with death threats from radical

Muslims. In 2004 she made a short film critical of Islam called Submission. The producer and director, Theo van Gogh, was subsequently stabbed to death by an Islamist, who called for a wider jihad against unbelievers in the West.

A further example is the widespread support among the liberal left for the Palestinian cause and antipathy towards the State of Israel. The purpose here is not to 'take sides', but simply to point out that Israel is a functioning democracy which among other things promotes the rights of women and gay people. In contrast, in the areas controlled by the Palestinian Authority and Hamas (the Gaza Strip) it is dangerous to be openly gay and the rights of women are poorly protected. In addition, freedom of speech, association, the press and religion are all curtailed.[20] In general terms, the values of the Israeli State are far closer to liberal Western values than those of the Palestinians and one might think that this would have some bearing on the attitude of the liberal left to the Palestinian issue, but this does not appear to be the case.

Hostility to Israel in the Labour Party has led to claims that it has a deep-seated problem with anti-Semitism. In 2016, the ex-Mayor of London Ken Livingstone and MP Naz Shah were both suspended from the party following alleged anti-Semitic comments[21] and Shami Chakrabarti was asked to launch a wider investigation into the issue within the Labour Party. In March 2018, the group Labour Against Anti-Semitism claimed that the problem was becoming institutionalised in the party and that the leadership was failing to deal effectively with allegations of anti-Semitism against party members.[22] Jeremy Corbyn, the Labour leader, was subsequently accused by the Board of Deputies of British Jews and the Jewish leadership Council of 'siding with anti-Semites'[23] and a demonstration was held outside Parliament by Jewish groups to protest over the issue.

These examples might lead us to ask how is it that the liberal left seems so enamoured with multiculturalism and keen to support groups whose cultural or religious practices run contrary to the values for which they claim to stand. This apparent contradiction is perplexing. Some have suggested that these attitudes are driven by guilt for past colonialism and imperialism. These historic crimes must be atoned for and the way to do that is to constantly criticise Western culture, blame all the world's problems on its past or present actions and not question the values of those who we used to 'oppress'; after all they are victims. More generally, the narrative of political correctness and post-modernism divides the world into oppressors and oppressed. Within a Western context, immigrant groups are more likely to be viewed as marginalised and oppressed and therefore in need of support, regardless of their own values.

The elephant in the room

In many ways multiculturalism has been the elephant in the room, particularly when it comes to Western society and the issue of tolerance. For various reasons, whether because of a sense of guilt about past colonialism and imperialism, a fear of racism, a desire not to be seen to be judging other cultures, or a concern for those who are considered to be oppressed, Western society has not wanted to talk about the obvious issues raised by the existence of multiple cultures in the same country. Following on from 9/11 and numerous other terrorist attacks throughout the Western world, this has all changed. Multiculturalism is out and social cohesion, shared values and integration are in; but the thorny question remains as to what extent the values and beliefs of immigrant communities should be tolerated when they clash with norms of wider Western culture.

References

1. Multiculturalism. (2017, July 19). In *Wikipedia, The Free Encyclopaedia*. Retrieved 09:16, July 20, 2017, from https://en.wikipedia.org/w/index.php?title=Multiculturalism&oldid=791259426. Licenced under CC-BY-SA 3.0. https://creativecommons.org/licenses/by-sa/3.0/

2. Forced Marriage Unit (2016), Retrieved August 29, 2017 from https://www.gov.uk/government/uploads/system/uploads/attachment_data/file/597869/Forced_Marriage_Unit_st

atistics-_2016.pdf. Contains public sector information
licensed under the Open Government Licence v3.0.

3. Female genital mutilation. Retrieved August 6, 2017
from http://www.nhs.uk/Conditions/female-genital-
mutilation/Pages/Introduction.aspx#why.

4. Honour killing (2017, July 13). In *Wikipedia, The
Free Encyclopaedia*. Retrieved 09:27, July 20, 2017
from,
https://en.wikipedia.org/w/index.php?title=Honor_killing
&oldid=790353932. Licenced under CC-BY-SA 3.0.
https://creativecommons.org/licenses/by-sa/3.0/

5. The depths of dishonour (2015, Dec). Retrieved Sept
12, 2017 from
https://www.justiceinspectorates.gov.uk/hmicfrs/wp-
content/uploads/the-depths-of-dishonour.pdf. Page 39.
Contains public sector information licensed under the
Open Government Licence v3.0.

6. Home Office (2016, May 26) Independent review into
sharia law launched. Retrieved July 28, 2017 from
https://www.gov.uk/government/news/independent-
review-into-sharia-law-launched. Contains public sector
information licensed under the Open Government
Licence v3.0.

7. Home Office (2016, May 26) Independent review into
sharia law launched. Retrieved July 28, 2017 from
https://www.gov.uk/government/news/independent-
review-into-sharia-law-launched. Contains public sector

information licensed under the Open Government Licence v3.0.

8. Evelyn Beatrice Hall. (2017, May 31). In *Wikipedia, The Free Encyclopaedia*. Retrieved 09:38, July 20, 2017, from https://en.wikipedia.org/w/index.php?title=Evelyn_Beatrice_Hall&oldid=783107671. Licenced under CC-BY-SA 3.0. https://creativecommons.org/licenses/by-sa/3.0/

9. Apostasy. (2017, August 29). In *Wikipedia, The Free Encyclopaedia*. Retrieved 14:45, September 1, 2017, from https://en.wikipedia.org/w/index.php?title=Apostasy&oldid=797802932.Licenced under CC-BY-SA 3.0. https://creativecommons.org/licenses/by-sa/3.0/

10. (2014, Nov 18). Christian Concern launches Safe Haven initiative. Retrieved July 20, 2017 from http://www.christianconcern.com/our-concerns/islam/christian-concern-launches-safe-haven-initiative-to-help-those-leaving-islam. Licenced under CC BY-ND 2.0 UK. https://creativecommons.org/licenses/by-nd/2.0/uk/

11. Cultural relativism. (2017, October 7). In *Wikipedia, The Free Encyclopaedia*. Retrieved 08:37, October 14, 2017 from https://en.wikipedia.org/w/index.php?title=Cultural_relativism&oldid=804195195Licenced under CC-BY-SA 3.0. https://creativecommons.org/licenses/by-sa/3.0/

12. Lewis, C.S., Mere Christianity (William Collins Sons and Co. Ltd. Glasgow, 1952)

13. Universal Declaration of Human Rights. Retrieved October 14, 2017 from http://www.un.org/en/universal-declaration-human-rights.

14. Cultural relativism. (2017, October 7). In *Wikipedia, The Free Encyclopaedia*. Retrieved 08:37, October 14, 2017 from https://en.wikipedia.org/w/index.php?title=Cultural_relativism&oldid=804195195 Licenced under CC-BY-SA 3.0. https://creativecommons.org/licenses/by-sa/3.0/

15. Johnston, P. (2006, Dec 9) Adopt our values or stay away. The Telegraph. Retrieved August 6, 2017 from http://www.telegraph.co.uk/news/uknews/1536408/Adopt-our-values-or-stay-away-says-Blair.html.

16. Speech at Munich Security Conference (2011, Feb 5). Retrieved July 28, 2017 from https://www.gov.uk/government/speeches/pms-speech-at-munich-security-conference. Contains public sector information licensed under the Open Government Licence v3.0.

17. German Election Results 2017. The Guardian. Retrieved October 17, 2017 from https://www.theguardian.com/world/ng-interactive/2017/sep/24/german-elections-2017-latest-results-live-merkel-bundestag-afd

18. Death penalty for homosexuality. (2017, August 17). In *Wikipedia, The Free Encyclopaedia*. Retrieved 19:58, August 24, 2017 from https://en.wikipedia.org/w/index.php?title=Death_penalty_for_homosexuality&oldid=795995896. Licenced under CC-BY-SA 3.0. https://creativecommons.org/licenses/by-sa/3.0/

19. (2007, Nov 27) My life under a fatwa. The Independent. Retrieved September 01, 2017 from http://www.independent.co.uk/news/people/profiles/ayaan-hirsi-ali-my-life-under-a-fatwa-760666.html.

20. Human rights in the State of Palestine. (2017, December 27). In *Wikipedia, The Free Encyclopaedia*. Retrieved 10:26, March 7, 2018, from https://en.wikipedia.org/w/index.php?title=Human_rights_in_the_State_of_Palestine&oldid=817298236. Licenced under CC-BY-SA 3.0. https://creativecommons.org/licenses/by-sa/3.0/

21. Taylor, A. (2016, April 29) Anti-Semitism. The Independent. Retrieved March 28, 2018 from https://www.independent.co.uk/news/uk/politics/labour-antisemitism-row-ken-livingstone-naz-shah-jeremy-corbyn-a7006176.html

22. Kentish, B. (2018, March 3) Anti-Semitism. The Independent. Retrieved March 7, 2018 from http://www.independent.co.uk/news/uk/politics/labour-antisemitism-disarray-compliance-jewish-ken-livingstone-jenny-formby-jeremy-corbyn-a8238541.html

23. Perkins, A. and Weaver, M. (2018, March 26) Jeremy Corbyn. The Guardian. Retrieved March 28, 2018 from https://www.theguardian.com/politics/2018/mar/26/jeremy-corbyn-accused-of-being-figurehead-for-antisemitism

Chapter 6: Towards a more tolerant society

In the previous chapters we have seen that there is a 'tolerance problem' in Western societies. Because of secularisation, globalisation, technological development and immigration, Western society is increasingly diverse and this makes it more difficult to agree on the boundaries of tolerance. In addition, we have shown that Western society is less tolerant than we perhaps thought. While the prevailing secular liberal consensus claims to have at its heart the notion of tolerance, this is in fact a myth. Rather there is a creeping intolerance that is seeking to silence and marginalise anyone who does not accept the liberal orthodoxy. Across the Western world most mainstream political parties appear to be signed up to this liberal agenda, though we noted the emergence of so called 'populist' parties and movements as a sign of growing opposition to the liberal consensus.

The purpose of this chapter is to stimulate some debate around the issue of tolerance and suggest some possible ways forward in dealing with the 'tolerance problem'. The slide towards intolerance is not inevitable and irreversible.

Sticking with the status quo – failing the tolerance test

It appears that going forward there are essentially two options when it comes to the issue of tolerance. Firstly, we can stick with the status quo, which means that those in power get to define the boundaries of tolerance and impose their values on everyone else. This is what the liberal fascists are trying to do. In the West, the general direction of travel has been towards a more secular and liberal society and therefore increasing intolerance towards those who do not share those beliefs. This approach is fine as long as we are prepared to live with the consequences. Society will be ever more fractured, divided and polarised; certain groups will be increasingly marginalised and discriminated against; otherwise law-abiding citizens, who have much to contribute to society, will be criminalised and excluded from the public space and valuable court time and public money will be wasted on dealing with 'thought crimes', rather than the criminal activity that really concerns the general public. In addition, public policy will increasingly be driven by ideology rather than by evidence, as those who would challenge the liberal orthodoxy are excluded from the public space.

The liberal fascists' approach to tolerance could be visually represented in the following diagram (figure 1). In the process of imposing the 'superior values' of liberalism, what we end up with is an ever-increasing area of enforced agreement in terms of values, belief and behaviour that everyone is supposed to sign up to. Issues that many would see as valid areas for disagreement are increasingly becoming areas where conformity to the liberal consensus is required. Outside of the limit of tolerance are those values and behaviours which the vast majority of people agree should not be tolerated and as such are not contentious.

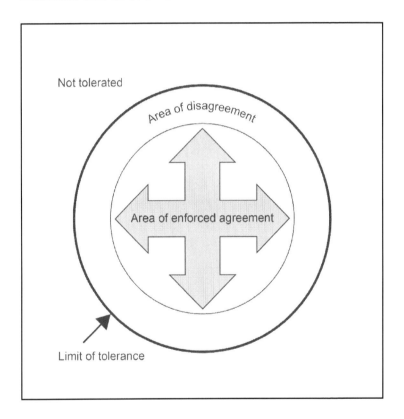

Figure 1. A diagrammatic representation of the liberal fascist approach to tolerance.

Towards a more tolerant society – some principles

Given the diverse, polarised and fragmented nature of Western societies, can we find a better way to live together that leads to less conflict, division, discrimination and intolerance? What alternative is there to the current situation where those in power are increasingly defining the boundaries of tolerance and imposing their values on the rest of us? In suggesting an alternative approach, we will start by outlining some general principles that will provide a foundation upon which to build our understanding of tolerance; these can also be used as guidelines to apply to any situation where the issue of tolerance arises. Having suggested some principles, we will then propose a model for tolerance and consider some of the issues that arise in its implementation.

Before going any further let us remind ourselves that tolerance is:

> A willingness to accept behaviour and beliefs that are different from your own, although you might not agree with or approve of them [1]

Tolerance implies that one group does not seek to force its values or beliefs on to another. To accept that someone can believe something but then stop them from acting on it is intolerant. Of course, there may be times when this is justified, but the point is that real tolerance isn't just about allowing other people to 'think something'! There is also an important distinction to be made between tolerance and agreement. Tolerance does not mean that we all must agree on everything, rather it is to do with how we handle our disagreements.

Accept difference

It goes without saying that the first principle we need to embrace if we want society to be tolerant is that we must accept some differences in behaviour and belief, especially in highly debateable and contentious areas of ethics and morality. This principle is in direct opposition to the attitude of the liberal fascists, who seek to impose conformity of behaviour and belief through political correctness and a variety of tactics including: the use of language, no platforming, safe spaces, equality and diversity policies, the creation of an artificial hierarchy of rights and intimidation.

At a practical level, the acceptance of difference means that in the current liberal climate it is okay to say you don't agree with gay marriage, that you believe abortion is wrong, or that you think gender is for the most part something that is binary and doesn't need to be questioned. It would mean that it is alright to state that you don't believe all cultural practises are equally valid and okay to discuss the merits or otherwise of different belief systems and faiths. It would mean it is acceptable to debate the issue of immigration and the impact that it is having on society. It would mean that people don't get fired by an employer just because they hold certain views that don't fit with the liberal orthodoxy.

Furthermore, accepting difference would mean that alternative views can be openly expressed in the public square, without fear, rather than having to be whispered in secret. The idea that someone should have to hide the fact that they are gay is nowadays seen as unacceptable, so why should it be any different for someone whose views are considered socially conservative? Non-liberals should be able to 'come out' and freely express their opinions. It should not have to be an issue for a politician like Tim Farron to say that he doesn't agree with gay sex,[2] particularly given that in doing so he probably reflects the views of millions of British people, who certainly back the right of politicians with traditional views to express them."[3]

Allow people to have their voices heard

Closely linked to the acceptance of difference is the second principle, that people must be allowed to have their voices heard. One of the hallmarks of a tolerant society is a determination to defend freedom of speech and an extreme reluctance to restrict it. In the words of Evelyn Beatrice Hall, which we have already quoted: "I disapprove of what you say, but I will defend to the death your right to say it".[4] Again this goes against the grain of political correctness, no platforming and safe spaces, which all seek to close-down freedom of expression. It challenges the use of language (phobias and name calling) as a way of silencing certain views. It means that the state should not be too hasty in bringing in laws to prevent people from expressing opinions with which it does not agree and that people should be able to say what they think without fear of intimidation and violence. It also means that people should be free to express opinions, even if others find them offensive. As soon as 'causing offence' is criminalised, free speech is effectively done away with, given that people can choose to be offended by any opinion that does not match their own!

Allowing people to express their opinion means that when an ex-Muslim like Maryam Namazie turns up at a university to address the issues of apostasy and blasphemy, she can do so, rather than being shouted down. It means when someone like the ex-magistrate Richard Page says that in his opinion it is not in the interests of a child to be adopted by a same-sex couple, he is listened to and what he says is weighed on the basis of the available evidence, rather than being reprimanded because his views don't happen to fit in with the current liberal consensus. It means that in all areas of life, including the professional and the public, an individual can express views and opinions based on the evidence, rather than on what is considered as politically correct.

We could add that there is an additional benefit to allowing people to express opinions, even though others might find them offensive. Views that are aired publicly can be debated and challenged. If they have merit, then that informs and benefits everyone; if they do not then they can be exposed for what they are.

Balancing rights

Thirdly, if tolerance is about accepting some differences and not seeking to impose one groups values on to others (particularly in contentious and debateable areas), then we can't have a situation in which the rights of some groups always trump those of others, yet we have seen numerous examples in this book of occasions where this has happened. In particular it appears that the priority for liberals is always the concept of 'equality'. Remember the words of Dame Louise Casey, Britain's Equalities Czar:

> "I have a problem with the expression 'religious conservatism,' because often it can be anti-equalities."[5]

This could be paraphrased as "we shouldn't take the views, values or rights of certain groups seriously because they don't correspond with our beliefs about equality." There appears to be a fundamental contradiction here. Equality demands that people should be treated equally in terms of their status, rights and opportunities, but if some groups are consistently favoured over others, then that would appear to be a clear case of inequality. A number of the examples we have looked at in this book, including the Asher's

Bakery case, the Green Party Councillor Ms Summers, the magistrate Richard Page, the relationships counsellor Gary McFarlane and the politician Tim Farron, all suggest that the rights of those who hold traditional views about marriage and human sexuality are seen as inferior to those who embrace the views of the current liberal orthodoxy. To claim that one group is anti-equality and then treat them unequally or assert that another is discriminatory and then discriminate against them appears to be a case of double standards.

At the same time, if equality is arbitrarily given more weight than other values which people hold to be important, such as freedom of religion, speech or conscience, then that is also an example of unequal treatment. Why should someone's right to have a cake decorated with particular words be deemed more important than another individual's right to be true to themselves, their conscience and their beliefs? In the sometimes-crazy world of liberal orthodoxy, it would appear that inequality is being created in the name of equality!

Where the interests or 'rights' of different groups are at odds with each other, a tolerant society will seek to balance the rights of those involved and accommodate them where possible, rather than simply impose the values of those in power. In most of the examples we have looked at where people were sacked from jobs, prevented from expressing opinions, or dragged before the courts for appearing to break equality laws, it would have been possible to accommodate the values and beliefs of the individuals involved. The fact that this didn't happen is testament to the intolerance of society.

The Asher's Bakery case should never have made it to court because the rights of the customer, who wanted a message supporting gay marriage, should have been balanced against those of the Bakers not to have to express an opinion that went against their beliefs. The customer could have gone to another shop or bought the cake from Asher's and had it decorated somewhere else. Unfortunately, it appears that the Equality Commission was more interested in promoting a particular ideology than ensuring equality and protecting the rights of both parties. In the case of the relationships counsellor, Gary McFarlane, one of have thought that it would be possible to accommodate his beliefs and values without compromising the service provided by his employer; a colleague could have provided counselling to same-sex couples. In both examples tolerance would have been an option, but intolerance was chosen instead.

Clearly there may be instances where it is not possible, or even reasonable, to balance and accommodate the preferences or rights of different groups or individuals. For example, someone working on a supermarket check-out has to accept that they need to handle alcohol and meat products; this is an integral part of the job that cannot be done by someone else. However, in a society that claims to value tolerance, the presumption should be that rights are accommodated and balanced where reasonably possible, particularly where issues of ethics and morality are concerned.

Evidence, reason and truth

Even in a tolerant society it is necessary to establish the boundaries of tolerance, so the last of our four principles is that this must be done on the basis of evidence, reason and truth, rather than ideology.

Before examining the relationship between truth and tolerance it is necessary to take a brief detour and ask what we mean by truth. This is a huge subject and worthy of a book in and of itself, so we can only touch on it briefly. In Western Europe during the period preceding the Enlightenment, the dominant worldview was that of Christianity. In Christian thought, truth is first and foremost something that is revealed by God. The 17th century Enlightenment saw the birth of modernism and a movement away from revelation as the primary source of truth, towards rationalism (human reason) and empiricism (verifiable knowledge acquired through the senses and experience). Truth was now to be sought after and discovered by the use of reason and the examination of evidence. Although these two means of seeking and understanding truth might seem 'miles apart', they were not that dissimilar. Both pre-modernists and modernists believed in the idea of objective truth, which could be discovered and known. In addition, while pre-modernists believed in revealed truth, they also used reason and evidence as a means of exploring and verifying that truth.

This all changed with the emergence of post-modernism in the mid-20th century. This challenged the idea of objective truth and instead viewed truth as being culturally located, relative and a matter of perception. Any claim to absolute truth was viewed with suspicion, as was the idea that it was possible to establish a 'meta-narrative' or overarching theory that could explain everything. Both were viewed as 'power plays' which had contributed to evils such as colonialism and totalitarianism, where one group imposed their values on to others.

So, which is it? Is truth objective, relative, or primarily a matter of perception? Can we use evidence and reason in order to discover truth, or are such efforts essentially futile? It matters to the subject of tolerance, because as we shall see, the use of reason to examine evidence is one of the main tools that society possesses in order to establish the boundaries of tolerance. The key argument for the existence of objective truth is that in most cases it is clearly apparent that truth exists independently of our perception and belief. At a mundane level we know this is so and everyday life would not be possible without accepting this premise. The classic example is that of a chair. If I sit on a chair, it will take my weight – assuming it isn't broken! This is an objective truth that does not rely on my beliefs or perception about the chair. The same is true even in areas where we can't be completely certain of the truth. Consider the question, "Is there life after death?" We cannot answer this question with the same level of certainty as the previous example regarding the chair, but there is still a 'true answer'. What happens after we die depends on what is true, not on our opinion.

So, how does the use of evidence and reason in the search for objective truth contribute to a tolerant society? It is no accident that intolerant societies are generally those which are either wedded to an authoritarian ideology or a personality cult that allows for no dissent. For these societies, truth is primarily located in ideology or personality, rather than being discovered through the examination of evidence and the use of reason. On the other hand, traditionally tolerant societies are ones that value the existence of different opinions. Through the process of discussion, debate and the use of evidence, these varied views can be examined and society can come to a considered opinion as to the best way forward in any given area of public policy. The two statements that follow are intended to illustrate the difference between these approaches to truth, in relation to the organisation of society:

"We believe X to be true. It is not open to question."

"We believe X to be true. However, this belief is open to question on the basis that evidence may come to light that requires it to be modified or abandoned."

The first statement is ideologically driven and intolerant. The truth is located in ideology and therefore beyond question; the evidence is actually irrelevant! We have seen in chapter 4 that political correctness falls into this category. Central to its ideology is the belief that all human history is defined and determined by power relationships between different groups. White heterosexual men are considered to have dominated power structures in the Western world for many centuries and to have been responsible for oppressing just about everyone else. PC is a reaction against this perceived concentration and abuse of power and is therefore concerned with redistributing power from the powerful to the powerless:

> Automatically opposing the powerful and supporting the powerless means that when presented with a new issue, the politically correct must decide not what is right or wrong, malign or benign, true or untrue, but who is the more powerful and who the less powerful.[6]

The problem is not that the PC narrative is without any merit, but rather that the ideology of oppression means that other evidence is not even considered. The truth of PC is not open to question. So, in the example of transgender people, this group has been oppressed in the past and must now be supported and affirmed, whatever the merit of their views, regardless of the evidence and the negative impact this may have on other groups in society.

The second of the two statements above reflects a society that values truth above ideology. In this case, evidence and reason are used to both develop and modify ideas and public policy. The underlying ideology not only allows for the existence of a diversity of opinion but considers this to be a strength. So again, to take the transgender issue, it is clear that while gender identity is a significant issue for a small minority of people, it is not something that troubles the vast majority of the population. While it is important to help the minority of people who struggle with gender dysphoria, there is no basis in evidence or reason to seek to impose an ideology on society that does away with the notion of gender or which encourages all children to question their gender identity.

Putting tolerance into practice in a diverse society

Setting out some basic principles of tolerance is comparatively easy; it is more difficult to work out how to apply these in practice. The following diagram (figure 2) illustrates a suggested model for how Western society could deal with the issue of tolerance.

At the centre of the diagram is the circle marked 'area of agreement'. This represents behaviour and belief that is almost universally accepted in society. Tolerance isn't an issue here because there is little if any dispute. How these values have arisen and the reason for their widespread acceptance is beyond the scope of this book.

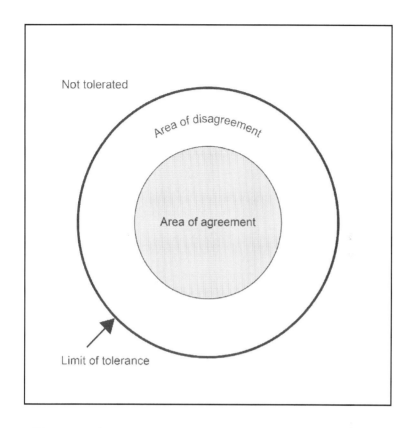

Figure 2. A suggested model for dealing with the issue of tolerance in Western society

The next circle represents areas of disagreement. This is behaviour and belief that some agree with and others don't. It is this area in which tolerance is required for different individuals and groups to get along with each other. At the outer edge of this circle is the 'limit of tolerance'. Beyond this are beliefs and behaviours that society overwhelmingly rejects. Again, while the reasons for this rejection may be obvious in most cases, it is not within the remit of this book to discuss the merits or otherwise of the behaviour or belief in this category.

The proposed model establishes the principle that in diverse Western societies there will not be unanimity on all issues and that within certain boundaries it is necessary to recognise differences of opinion and find ways of enabling people to live together with those disagreements. It may help to flesh this out a little by suggesting some examples of behaviour and belief that might be found in each area of the model.

Area of agreement: this is behaviour and belief that is generally accepted as okay in Western society. It would include the need to respect the rule of law, to pay taxes in order to support public services, to follow the rules of the road, to queue up and not push in (at least in the UK!), to resolve disagreements peacefully rather than through the use of violence, to accept the right of others to hold different political views, to accept the result of democratic elections even if you don't like them, to pay for things rather than steal them and to treat others with respect regardless of their race, colour, age, gender, religion or sexual orientation, etc. Of course, there will be some variation between different groups in society as to the acceptance of these norms and there will be some people in every society who reject them.

Areas of disagreement: these are areas of valid disagreement that are driven by culture, religion, ethics and politics. They would include such things as: the nature and purpose of human sexuality and marriage, our understanding of gender, various areas of medical ethics such as experimentation on human embryos, euthanasia and abortion, immigration, the role of religion in society, the boundaries of free speech, the role and extent of the welfare state and the importance or otherwise of certain environmental issues, etc.

Beyond the limit of tolerance: this is behaviour and belief that society almost universally believes should not be tolerated. This would include: murder, racism, paedophilia, drink-driving, domestic violence, child abuse, cruelty to animals, theft, fraud, modern-day slavery, honour crimes and forced marriage, etc. Again, while most people would reject these attitudes and behaviours, there are some who do not, hence the need for criminal justice systems!

The tolerance rule

Having outlined some general principles that underpin our idea of tolerance and proposed a model for how Western society might deal with the issue, we are in a position to suggest a general rule for tolerance: "*In areas where there is significant disagreement in society, we seek to apply the four principles of tolerance: we accept difference, we allow people to express their views openly, we seek to balance the rights of different groups in society and we establish the boundaries of tolerance on the basis of truth, evidence and reason.*"

What are the boundaries of tolerance?

Two obvious questions arise from the model that we have suggested. Firstly, what are the boundaries of tolerance and secondly, who defines those boundaries?

Numbers matter

In a democratic society, it would be natural to assume that part of the criteria for deciding if a particular belief or behaviour should fall within the boundary of tolerance is the number of people who subscribe to it. If a large enough group believe that X or Y is a valid belief or behaviour, then a democratic society would need to think carefully before placing it outside of the boundary of tolerance. However, there are a number of difficulties with this approach.

The first problem is that if the boundaries of tolerance are simply decided on the basis of numbers, this could easily lead to the tyranny of the majority, which we have already referred to in chapter 1. The values and beliefs of a minority could be placed outside the boundary of tolerance simply because they do not tally with those of the majority, rather than because they are damaging or there is anything intrinsically wrong with them.

The second problem arises from the nature of liberal Western democracies and their justifiable concern to prevent the tyranny of the majority. This combined with the influence of political correctness and the rise of identity politics has led to a situation where fashionable and vocal minorities appear to have more influence than their numbers justify. The tyranny of the majority is substituted for the tyranny of the vocal minority. In 2016 there were estimated to be about 650,000 people in the UK who are "likely to be gender incongruent to some degree",[7] which is about 1% of the population. In 2015, the Annual Population Survey found 1.7% of adults in the UK identified themselves as lesbian, gay or bisexual.[8] Despite being a small percentage of the population, we have seen that the LGBT lobby wields enormous influence. In comparison, according to the English Church census of 2005, 6.5% of the population of England attended church regularly and 40% of these attended evangelical churches,[9] which would mean that approximately 2.6% of the English population are evangelical Christians. Given those numbers, one would assume that their views and opinions should be accorded the same respect and tolerance as those of gay and transgender people, but we have seen that this is not the case. Some minorities are less fashionable than others.

The third problem is that we could foresee a situation where certain areas of belief or behaviour would have to be tolerated despite most of the population finding them unacceptable. If enough people believed that forced marriage or a ban on apostasy (converting to another religion) was acceptable, then in a democratic system there would be pressure on the government to make such practises legal, despite opposition from the majority.

Core values matter

It is clear then that while numbers are important in helping a democratic society to decide on the boundaries of tolerance, they are not sufficient in and of themselves. We need some additional measures against which belief and behaviour can be evaluated. This is where the idea of British or Western values is useful. Behaviour or belief that clearly contradicts any of these core values would most likely be considered unacceptable. It is beyond the scope of this book to examine the origin and validity of these values; we simply note that they exist and that they represent core beliefs that Western society considers to be both foundational and non-negotiable.

However, as we saw earlier, the problem with the current attempt to apply 'British values' is that the rule of law (or at least the way the law is interpreted) often works against the 'mutual respect and tolerance of other faiths and beliefs'; one core value is in effect nullifying another. If we are to live in a tolerant society, this inherent contradiction needs to be overcome. The law needs to work for tolerance, not against it. This could be achieved quite simply by seeking to balance the rights of different groups and by doing away with the artificial hierarchy of values that allows equality to always win out over other values such as freedom of belief, conscience and speech.

So, if we take the four core British values of democracy, the rule of law, individual liberty and mutual respect and tolerance of those with different faiths and beliefs as a starting point, it is evident that certain beliefs and behaviours are incompatible with these values. Forced marriage is not tolerated because it contradicts the value of individual liberty; in this case the right of an individual to decide if and who they should marry. Similarly, Western society rejects the idea that an individual should not be permitted to change their faith or worldview, because this is also a matter of individual liberty. In both cases core values are being violated and so tolerance of these beliefs or behaviours is inappropriate. Another example from the UK is the banning of certain political groups on the basis that they incite violence, hatred and intolerance towards others in society. The proscribed organisations include many that are Islamist, as well as others from the extreme right and left of the political spectrum.[10] The aims and methods of these groups breach most core Western values and therefore they are not tolerated.

Where there are differences in belief and behaviour that do not violate any of the core values, the presumption should be that of tolerance. Given the caveat that the law should seek to balance the rights of different groups in society and not automatically place equality above freedom of belief, speech and conscience, there is no reason why most of the areas of disagreement that have been alluded to in this book, should be considered to sit outside of the boundary of tolerance. For example, the law in the UK allows people of the same sex to marry and to engage in homosexual relationships. At the same time, it does not seek to force a particular definition of marriage or human sexuality upon its citizens. Holding traditional views that marriage and sexual relationships should be between men and women does not curtail the rights of same sex couples to marry, interfere with the liberty of others, break the law or necessarily indicate a lack of mutual respect and tolerance. Let us remember that tolerance does not equate to agreement. As such, this belief does not breach any core British values and should be viewed as a belief/behaviour that sits inside the area of disagreement.

In a society that claims to be tolerant, it is therefore wrong that a Christian student could be removed from a social work course at a university for simply expressing the view on Facebook that homosexuality and same sex marriage is 'sinful'. Yet this is what happened to Felix Ngole who was studying at Sheffield University.[11] During the court case that followed, the Barrister for the university argued that his views could undermine the trust and confidence that gay clients might have in him. However, exactly the same could be said for a social worker who expressed support for gay marriage and then worked with a family or individual who had more traditional values. Indeed, if we took this argument to its logical conclusion, no one who ever expressed a view about a controversial or debateable subject on social media would ever be able to enter the profession. All social workers will hold personal views that could potentially conflict with those of the clients they are working with, but this does not make them unfit for the job. Mutual respect and tolerance does not require agreement with others as to what they believe.

Similarly, the law in most of the UK allows women to have abortions, the exception being Northern Ireland, where the restrictions on abortion reflect different cultural attitudes. There are however many people who believe that for the most part the practice is immoral and unethical. Some of these people work in medical fields and exercise their right to not take part in such procedures. Again, no core British values are breached and this is another area that should be viewed as one of legitimate disagreement. Women who want an abortion are at liberty to have one, within the limits of the law and those who have moral objections to assisting with the practice, have the liberty not to be involved. The rights of the two groups are respected and balanced.

If we ever found ourselves in the situation where it was illegal to express the view that marriage should be between a man and a woman, or where medical professionals were forced to take part in abortion procedures, we would in effect be living in a fascist state and this book would be redundant as well as probably on some banned list!

However, it isn't always that simple to determine if core Western values are being violated. For example, several European countries, including Belgium, France and Austria have banned the wearing of the burqa (full veil) and niqab (face covering that just reveals the eyes) in public places and the European Court of Justice (ECJ) has ruled that employers have the right to stop employees wearing visible religious symbols, including Muslim head coverings.[12] Some may argue that this is a betrayal of the principle of individual liberty and of tolerance towards those of different faiths. For others it is a necessary step to liberate women from oppression, to protect the public from criminals and terrorists seeking to conceal their identity, to promote social cohesion and to remove barriers to communication. Qanta Ahmed, a British Muslim physician, author and newspaper columnist, has written in support of the ECJ ruling on the right of employers to ban the wearing of the veil, on the basis that radical Islam is a threat to the social cohesion of European countries.[13] She argues that Islamists thrive on the idea of Muslims being a 'society within a society' and that enforcing dress codes based on religion promotes their sectarian agenda.

Another example is that of the Al-Hijrah Islamic school in Birmingham, which in October 2017 was found to be acting unlawfully by substantially segregating boys and girls from the age of nine, teaching them in different classrooms and making them use different playgrounds and corridors.[14] The systematic segregation of children by gender, within the same school, is certainly alien to modern Western culture but does it breach any core British values? One of the main arguments against the practice is that if fails to prepare pupils for life in modern Britain, where people are generally not segregated based on their sex; this is again an issue to do with social cohesion. However, the concern of the Appeal Court seemed to be more to do with discrimination based on gender; in which case we are back to the question of the equalities agenda and its relationship to tolerance of those with different faiths and beliefs. What these two examples illustrate is that while core Western values are a useful tool in helping us to decide whether something should be tolerated, they do not always provide us with an adequate and unambiguous measure.

Evidence matters

Given the problems we have identified with both numbers and core Western values in establishing the boundaries of tolerance, there is another important tool that we can use - empirical evidence. Whether a particular belief or behaviour should be tolerated, ought to depend in part upon the evidence as to its harm or benefit. This assumes that we wish to prevent people harming themselves or others and that we believe in the use of evidence and reason as tools to discern the best course of action to take.

In the examples we have just examined regarding the wearing of certain head coverings and segregation of the sexes within the same school, the argument of some would be that these practices damage social cohesion and therefore are harmful to society. As such it would be right to 'breach' the core value of tolerance for the greater good of social cohesion and integration. Perhaps a less controversial example would be that of smoking. As a society, we no longer tolerate smoking in public buildings due to the overwhelming evidence that it damages people's health. Smoking hasn't been banned, but the rights of smokers have been curtailed for the benefit of non-smokers. While it may be more difficult to apply this principle to such contentious issues as human sexuality, gender identity, medical ethics, abortion, climate change or the role of religion in Western society, it should be both possible and desirable to look at the available evidence when considering the acceptability or otherwise of certain values or beliefs. Where the evidence of harm or benefit is unclear, we should be reluctant to pick sides and marginalise certain viewpoints. Where the evidence is clear, we should be willing to follow where it leads and not allow people to be silenced simply because their opinions are unfashionable. Of course, the problem with evidence is that people tend to select that which supports their preconceived views and ignore that which may contradict what they want to believe. Facts and truth are often subordinated to ideology or conveniently manipulated to serve a political purpose.

The 'hurt test'

For many people, the ultimate test of the acceptability of a particular value or viewpoint is what we could call the 'hurt test'. If no one gets hurt as a result, then it is okay. At one level this works quite well as most of the things we outlaw as a society are activities or attitudes which cause obvious harm to others or to ourselves. However, the application of this principle is inconsistent and evidence of harm is sometimes ignored if the behaviour and values are ideologically driven.

For example, abortion is clearly harmful to unborn children, who are conveniently relabelled as 'products of conception' to avoid any uncomfortable prodding of the conscience. It is often the case that within the same hospital, unborn babies are being killed in one department, while everything is being done to save them in another. When the unborn are wanted they are treated as children and patients, when they are unwanted they are treated in the same way as a 'cancer' that needs to be removed. The moral contradiction should be obvious. There is also evidence of potential harm to the adults involved. Alongside the well-known physical problems and side effects associated with having an abortion, many women also suffer from an increased risk of mental health problems following the procedure[15] and there is also a growing recognition that the husbands or partners of women having abortions can suffer similar problems.[16] The evidence of harm is clear, but it is ignored because the 'woman's right to choose' is an ideological absolute for liberals.

Another example is sex education policy in the UK. In March 2017, the government announced that sex and relationships education (SRE) would be made compulsory in all schools, whereas previously this was only the case in those run by local authorities. All children from the age of four upwards will be taught about safe and healthy relationships.[17] The news was welcomed by the Local Government Association (LGA), which had been campaigning for compulsory sex education in all schools. In a statement following the announcement, the LGA said that it believed that the lack of compulsory SRE in all secondary schools was creating a 'ticking sexual health time bomb' and that making it compulsory would help to reduce the high number of STI (sexually transmitted infections) diagnosis in young people as well as prepare them for adulthood and enable them to better take care of themselves and future partners.[18] However, the evidence about the benefits or otherwise of sex education is far from conclusive. A recent international review published in November 2016 found that:

> Sex education does not reduce the rate of teenage pregnancy or incidences of sexually transmitted infections (STIs). A comprehensive Cochrane review of studies from around the world combined the data from more than 55,000 young people, aged on average between 14 and 16.[19]

Another study by academics at Nottingham University, this time looking at the UK government's attempts to reduce teenage pregnancies found that:

> The fall in teenage pregnancies in the UK can be linked to funding cuts for sexual health services, according to new research. The changes meant less advertising for services and made contraceptives less readily available. The findings have been described as a 'wake-up call' to those who continue to claim such services are needed to reduce teen pregnancies. Professor David Paton and Research Assistant Liam Wright found that the Government's provision of contraception and its sex advice services may have encouraged risky behaviour, rather than curbed it. Between 1999 and 2010 the Government ran the Teenage Pregnancy Strategy. Under the strategy, hundreds of millions of pounds were spent on contraceptive services and sex and relationships education. The scheme concluded in 2010, leading to warnings by some, including the Teenage Pregnancy Independent Advisory Group, that teenage pregnancy would rise if there were cuts to funding. However, Prof Paton said: "Contrary to expectations, we found that, if anything, cuts have led to fewer teen pregnancies." The study went as far as to say that "spending on projects related to teenage pregnancy may even be counterproductive".[20]

At best the evidence seems to suggest that the benefits of sex education may be mixed, at worst it may indicate that giving young people explicit information about sex and access to contraceptives simply encourages them to engage in sexual activity and therefore put themselves at risk of unwanted pregnancy or sexually transmitted disease; in other words, it may be harmful. The fact that the government seems determined to push on with its sex education agenda in schools would suggest that either it isn't looking at the evidence, or that it is primarily motivated by ideology and a desire to 'educate' children in liberal values regarding human sexuality.

The other issue with the principle of harm is that the evidence for it needs to be objective, rather than subjective. For example, most convinced atheists seem to consider religious faith to be harmful to individuals and society and you don't need to look too far on the web to find people arguing that it should be banned, or at the very least kept private! However, this goes against the evidence, which is much more mixed. There is a wealth of research which has tied being religious with better well-being and overall mental health, as well as research that has indicated the potential harm of particular religious beliefs.[21] Faith has done much good in the world, as well as harm and to seek to generally restrict it would be driven by ideology rather than supported by objective evidence.

Deciding on the boundaries of tolerance is not always easy, but by applying the four general principles of tolerance and considering the numbers of people involved, core Western values and the evidence of benefit or harm, it should be possible to establish the boundaries in a methodical and rational manner, rather than simply on the basis of personal or group prejudice.

Who decides on the boundaries?

The other question this model throws up is that of who decides on the boundaries of tolerance? In democratic societies, the normal model of government is that the people elect representatives, who govern on their behalf. In theory this ought to mean that those who govern reflect the will of the majority of the governed. However, as we have already seen in chapter 4, democratic systems have a number of major flaws.

Firstly, depending on the method of electing governments, those in power often fail to reflect the views of a sizeable portion of the electorate; this is particularly true in a first past the post electoral system such as the one that we have in the UK. Secondly, when people vote for a party at an election, they usually don't agree with all of its policies. Indeed, on occasions they may well be voting for a party on the basis that it is the 'least worst option', or that it will keep an even less desirable alternative out of government. Thirdly, we have already noted that as all the main political parties in the UK have adopted more socially liberal attitudes, those who consider themselves socially conservative have in effect been disenfranchised. No main-stream party now reflects their views on certain social issues that they feel strongly about. So, the idea that a party has a mandate for all its policies because it has been voted into government is clearly false.

There are a number of possible solutions to this democratic deficit, but they all have their own flaws. A system of proportional representation would give everyone who votes more of an opportunity to have their voice heard and in this sense it is far superior to the first past the post method in reflecting the 'will of the people'. The 12.6% of the UK population who voted UKIP in the 2015 general election would have received proper representation, instead of the one MP that they ended up with (out of 650), which was clearly unfair. The downside of this system is that minority parties are sometimes able to obtain a larger say in making policy than their support justifies, because a larger party requires their backing to govern. Proportional systems can also be politically less stable, leading to more frequent changes in government and greater difficulty in forming one in the first place. Another option would be to have more referenda as a way of giving everyone entitled to vote a say on controversial legislation. The philosophical problem with this approach is deciding on what level of support is required for a decision to be taken; if it is simply anything over 50% that wins the day, then all a referendum does it show how divided society is. If it is something higher, like 60%, you may be in danger of never doing anything because you can't get sufficient votes. There is also an economic issue at play, in terms of the cost of running more referenda.

It is probably too much to hope for, but perhaps the best solution would be that governments and those who derive their authority from them, recognise the limits of their democratic mandate and seek to govern in the interests of the whole population, not just those who reflect their own views. Controversial legislation would only be introduced after extensive consultation and careful examination of the evidence. Where there were a variety of valid viewpoints, these would be accommodated.

No doubt the UK government and devolved administrations would claim that they already do this, but in reality 'consultation' and 'careful examination of the evidence' too often appears to be little more than a public relations exercise, the outcome of which has already been decided. We have already noted an example of this in chapter 4, where we looked at the Scottish government's attempt to bring in a scheme whereby each child would have a named state guardian. This was after consultation and in the face of significant opposition from parents and a variety of organisations which saw it as unwarranted interference by the state in family life. In a poll by ComRes commissioned by opponents to the scheme, 64% of Scots were against the move and only 24% thought that the named person could always be trusted to act in the child's best interests.[22] Despite this opposition, the Scottish government went ahead with its proposals, which might lead us to conclude that they were never that concerned about what the Scottish people thought, or inclined to listen to the arguments of those who opposed the idea.

There are also a number of other issues with the process of government consultation. Firstly, there is the very real danger that due to the dominance of secular liberal thinking within most of society's institutions, consultation becomes an exercise in 'groupthink'. This is:

> A psychological phenomenon that occurs within a group of people in which the desire for harmony or conformity in the group results in an irrational or dysfunctional decision-making outcome. Group members try to minimize conflict and reach a consensus decision without critical evaluation of alternative viewpoints by actively suppressing dissenting viewpoints, and by isolating themselves from outside influences.[23]

Essentially if a group of people all think the same, they are unlikely to make good decisions, since there is no one to challenge their ideas or suggest alternative viewpoints.

Secondly, the extent to which politicians are willing to consult and listen is directly correlated to the size of their majority in parliament. Those with small majorities are likely to be 'conservative' in their policy ambitions and more inclined to build alliances, listen and consult, whereas those with large majorities tend to simply drive through their policies. Thirdly, in respect of their policies, democratic politicians often want to 'have their cake and eat it'. If the public supports a particular policy, then the government of the day claims to be listening; if the public opposes the same policy then the government claims to be 'providing leadership!' Fourthly, if policy decisions are ideologically driven, governments are unlikely to listen to alternative viewpoints, as we saw in the case of the named person's scheme. Lastly, we have already noted in an earlier chapter that the democratic process can be highjacked by fashionable and vocal minorities who manage to persuade the government to adopt their agendas. In such a climate, government is less likely to listen to unfashionable groups who are proposing an alternative viewpoint.

Safeguarding Tolerance

While liberal democracy provides us with the best chance we have of creating a tolerant society, it is clear that there is no automatic link between democracy and tolerance. The UK is a well-established liberal democracy, has an independent judiciary, as well as a media that is for the most part free of government control and yet this has not been sufficient to prevent the creeping intolerance of liberal fascism. Given this fact, it seems that extra safeguards need to be put in place to promote tolerance, limit the power of the state, protect minorities and prevent the 'tyranny of the majority' or the 'vocal minority'.

In the UK, people's fundamental rights are supposed to be protected by the Human Rights Act of 1998, which takes 16 of the fundamental rights in the European Convention of Human Rights and pulls them down into domestic law.[24] However, it appears that this does not provide adequate protection for those whose beliefs and values are out of sync with the liberal orthodoxy. While the Human Rights Act provides for the right to freedom of expression, thought, conscience and religion, it did not provide protection for Asher's Bakery who refused to decorate a cake with a message that went against their own beliefs and values. Neither did it stop Felix Ngole from being expelled from a social work course for expressing traditional views on homosexuality,[25] or losing his subsequent appeal against the decision.[26] While recognising that rights need to be balanced with responsibilities and against those of other groups, it seems that the Human Rights Act isn't working when it comes to protecting those who have the audacity to oppose the liberal orthodoxy. The main problem appears to be that the rights enshrined in it are subjected to numerous caveats and qualifications, the result of which is an expansion of the power of the state at the cost of the individual.[27] For example, Article 10 of the Act which deals with freedom of expression reads as follows:

> Everyone has the right to freedom of expression. This right shall include freedom to hold opinions

and to receive and impart information and ideas without interference by public authority and regardless of frontiers. This Article shall not prevent States from requiring the licensing of broadcasting, television or cinema enterprises.

The exercise of these freedoms, since it carries with it duties and responsibilities, may be subject to such formalities, conditions, restrictions or penalties as are prescribed by law and are necessary in a democratic society, in the interests of national security, territorial integrity or public safety, for the prevention of disorder or crime, for the protection of health or morals, for the protection of the reputation or rights of others, for preventing the disclosure of information received in confidence, or for maintaining the authority and impartiality of the judiciary.[28]

In effect the Act says, "You have the right to freedom of expression, but the government can legitimately restrict that freedom for a whole variety of reasons." In this sense the Human Rights Act is fundamentally illiberal and it is easy to see how it can be used by those in government to impose their own values and beliefs on to wider society. Those whose views are out of sync with the authorities are unable to appeal to the Act for protection, because the rights and freedoms enshrined in it can simply be 'interpreted away' on the basis of its many caveats and qualifications. We have seen numerous examples in this book where the right to freedom of thought, conscience and religion appears to be meaningless, if the beliefs expressed do not conform to the current liberal consensus.

If we really believe in tolerance and fundamental human rights, then it seems that we require a stronger legal framework enshrined in a bill of rights or written constitution, to promote tolerance, limit the power of the state and protect minorities. Perhaps what we need is an equivalent to the First Amendment to the US Constitution, which is qualification free and all about limiting the power of those in authority:

> Congress shall make no law respecting an establishment of religion or prohibiting the free exercise thereof; or abridging the freedom of speech, or of the press; or the right of the people peaceably to assemble, and to petition the Government for a redress of grievances.[29]

References

1. The Online Cambridge Dictionary; 2017. Retrieved July 28, 2017 from http://dictionary.cambridge.org/dictionary/english/Tolerance.

2. Tolhurst, A. (2017, April 23) Tim Farron under fire. The Sun. Retrieved July 28, 2017 from https://www.thesun.co.uk/news/3393817/tim-farron-under-fire-over-his-views-on-homosexuality-again-after-lib-dem-leader-refuses-to-say-if-gay-sex-is-a-sin/.

3. (2017, April 27) Brits back rights of MPs to say 'gay sex is a sin'. Retrieved August 7, 2017 from http://www.christian.org.uk/news/brits-back-right-mps-say-gay-sex-sin/?e280417.

4. Evelyn Beatrice Hall. (2017, May 31). In *Wikipedia, The Free Encyclopaedia*. Retrieved09:38, July 20, 2017, from https://en.wikipedia.org/w/index.php?title=Evelyn_Beatrice_Hall&oldid=783107671. Licenced under CC-BY-SA 3.0. https://creativecommons.org/licenses/by-sa/3.0/

5. Religious conservatism (2017, Jan 13) Retrieved Jan 11, 2017 from http://www.christianconcern.com/our-concerns/dame-louise-casey-religious-conservatism-is-often-anti-equalities

6. Browne, A., The Retreat of Reason: Political correctness and the corruption of public debate in modern Britain (Civitas, 2006) page 11.

7. (2016, Jan). Transgender Equality. First Report of Session 2015-2016. Retrieved August 26, 2017 from https://publications.parliament.uk/pa/cm201516/cmselect/cmwomeq/390/390.pdf

8. (2016, Oct 5) Sexual identity: UK 2015. Retrieved August 7, 2017 from https://www.ons.gov.uk/peoplepopulationandcommunity/culturalidentity/sexuality/bulletins/sexualidentityuk/2015. Contains public sector information licensed under the Open Government Licence v3.0.

9. (2008, March 20) English Church census 2005. Retrieved August 7, 2017 from http://www.eauk.org/church/research-and-statistics/english-church-census.cfm.

10. (2017, Dec) Proscribed Terrorist organisations. Retrieved January 25, 2018 from https://www.gov.uk/government/uploads/system/uploads/attachment_data/file/670599/20171222_Proscription.pdf

11. Rudgard, O. (2017, April 25) High Court to rule. Retrieved August 7, 2017 from http://www.telegraph.co.uk/news/2017/04/25/high-court-rule-christian-student-declared-unfit-practice-social/.

12. European Court. (2015, March 14) Retrieved Oct 21, 2017 from https://www.premier.org.uk/News/World/European-court-allows-religious-symbol-ban

13. Qanta, A. (2017, March 18) As a Muslim. The Spectator. Retrieved Oct 21, 2017 from https://www.spectator.co.uk/2017/03/the-right-to-ban-the-veil-is-good-news-for-everybody-including-muslims/

14. Adams, R. (2017, Oct 30) Islamic School gender segregation. Retrieved October 20, 2017 from https://www.theguardian.com/education/2017/oct/13/islamic-school-gender-segregation-unlawful-court-of-appeal

15. Coleman, P.K. (2011) Abortion and mental health. Retrieved August 26, 2017 from

http://bjp.rcpsych.org/content/bjprcpsych/199/3/180.full.p
df

16. Effects for men. Retrieved August 7, 2017 from
http://www.postabortionpaths.org.nz/MenAbortion/Effec
tsMen.asp.

17. Sellgren, K. (2017, March 1) Sex education to be
compulsory. Retrieved July 20, 2017 from
http://www.bbc.co.uk/news/education-39116783.

18. (2017, Feb 1) LGA responds to SRE announcement,
Retrieved August 7, 2017 from
https://www.local.gov.uk/about/news/lga-responds-sex-
and-relationship-education-announcement

19. (2016, Nov 10) Sex education does not reduce teen
pregnancy. Retrieved August 6, 2017 from
http://www.christianconcern.com/our-
concerns/education/sex-education-does-not-reduce-teen-
pregnancy-or-stis-review-finds.

20. (2017, June 2) Teenage Pregnancy Fall. Retrieved
October 31, 2017 from
http://www.christian.org.uk/news/teenage-pregnancy-
fall-linked-funding-cuts/

21. Rettner, R. (2015, Sept 23) God help us? Retrieved
July 28, 2017 from https://www.livescience.com/52197-
religion-mental-health-brain.html.

22. Macnab, S. (2016, March 28) Majority of Scots against. The Scotsman. Retrieved Oct 20, 2017 from http://www.scotsman.com/news/politics/majority-of-scots-against-intrusive-named-person-proposals-1-4083863

23. Groupthink. (2017, October 24). In *Wikipedia, The Free Encyclopedia*. Retrieved 17:55, October 24, 2017, from https://en.wikipedia.org/w/index.php?title=Groupthink&oldid=806843206. Licenced under CC-BY-SA 3.0. https://creativecommons.org/licenses/by-sa/3.0/

24. The Human Rights Acts. Retrieved Nov 3, 2017 from https://www.bihr.org.uk/thehumanrightsact

25. Rudgard, O. (2017, April 25) High Court to rule. Retrieved August 7, 2017 from http://www.telegraph.co.uk/news/2017/04/25/high-court-rule-christian-student-declared-unfit-practice-social/.

26. Grierson, J. (2017, October 27, 2017) Christian thrown out. The Guardian. Retrieved Nov 3, 2017 from https://www.theguardian.com/uk-news/2017/oct/27/christian-felix-ngole-thrown-out-sheffield-university-anti-gay-remarks-loses-appeal

27. (2015, May 19) The First Amendment. Retrieved Nov 3, 2017 from http://www.spiked-online.com/newsite/article/the-first-amendment-vs-the-human-rights-act/16986#.Wfy4wPmLTcu

28. Human Rights Act 1998. Retrieved Nov 7, 2017 from http://www.legislation.gov.uk/ukpga/1998/42/schedule/1/ part/I/chapter/9. Open Government Licence v3.0

29. First Amendment to the United States Constitution. (2017, October 16). In *Wikipedia, The Free Encyclopaedia*. Retrieved 18:23, November 3, 2017, from https://en.wikipedia.org/w/index.php?title=First_A mendment_to_the_United_States_Constitution&oldid=8 05640275. https://creativecommons.org/licenses/by-sa/3.0/

Chapter 7: Conclusion

Western society has a tolerance problem. As it becomes increasingly diverse, it is more difficult to establish the boundaries of tolerance and at the same time the largely secular liberal authorities are becoming increasingly intolerant of anyone who does not sign up to the liberal consensus.

The liberals' claim to be the champions of tolerance is a myth. While loudly proclaiming their opposition to intolerance in the forms of Islamophobia, transphobia, homophobia and racism etc., the liberal fascists have plenty of 'phobias' of their own. Liberalism has morphed from a philosophy that assumed the right to differ, into a form of fascism that is intolerant of anyone who expresses views that are outside of the liberal orthodoxy. While claiming to believe in liberal principles such as tolerance, liberty, the importance of equality, social justice and the rights of the individual, so-called liberals are seeking to impose their values upon the rest of us, denying these very principles. There is nothing progressive about taking society back to a time when people were marginalised, discriminated against and effectively criminalised, simply for expressing views that differ from those in authority.

The liberal fascists are using a variety of tactics in their quest to recreate society in their own image. Political correctness, the use of language, equality and diversity policies, no platforming and safe spaces, the instruments of the state, celebrity culture, the media and intimidation are all being used to impose liberal values and marginalise those who cannot or will not sign up to the liberal orthodoxy. This has damaging consequences for both the individuals who bear the impact and cost of intolerance, as well as for wider society. As alternative viewpoints are silenced, public policy decisions are increasingly subject to 'group think' and driven by ideology, rather than reason and evidence. Liberal democracy is undermined by changing the balance of power between the state and the individual and some minorities are promoted while others are marginalised. Social cohesion is also damaged as groups which consider themselves victimised seek to use the power of the state to remedy their situation, usually at the expense of others.

Those who hold liberal views and who are part of the liberal establishment have a choice to make, either to carry on down the path of liberal fascism, or to rediscover the roots of liberalism and genuinely embrace the tolerance that they claim to espouse. If they choose to continue their present course, they should at least have the honesty to stop pretending and admit that they don't really believe in tolerance at all, but rather in the superiority of their own values, which they wish to impose upon the rest of society in the interests of so-called modernity and progress.

To choose the path of tolerance is undoubtedly difficult in the increasingly diverse Western societies in which we live; however, the model that has been suggested gives us a framework in which to do this. While recognising that tolerance has its boundaries and suggesting some ways in which these could be established, we must acknowledge that there are valid areas of disagreement in society that should be accommodated. By accepting difference, protecting freedom of speech, balancing the rights of different groups and using evidence and reason to establish boundaries, we can ensure that Western society continues to be one that is marked by the characteristic of tolerance.

The last word goes to Tim Farron, who resigned as leader of the Liberal Democrats on June 14th, 2017, following continued criticism of his traditional Christian views on homosexuality. His experience highlights just how intolerant our society has become, but at the same time his resignation speech points us towards what it means to be truly tolerant. He said:

> To be a political leader - especially of a progressive, liberal party in 2017 - and to live as a committed Christian, to hold faithfully to the Bible's teaching, has felt impossible for me. I'm a liberal to my fingertips and that liberalism means that I am passionate about defending the rights and liberties of people who believe different things to me. There are Christians in politics who take the view that they should impose the tenets of faith on society, but I have not taken that

approach because I disagree with it - it's not liberal and it is counterproductive when it comes to advancing the gospel. Even so, I seem to be the subject of suspicion because of what I believe and who my faith is in. In which case we are kidding ourselves if we think we yet live in a tolerant, liberal society.[1]

References

1. (2017, June 14) Tim Farron resigns. Retrieved August 8, 2017 from http://www.libdems.org.uk/liberal-democrat-leader-tim-farron-resigns#.

Picture credits

Figure 1. A diagrammatic representation of the liberal fascist approach to tolerance. Andy Brown

Figure 2. A suggested model for dealing with the issue of tolerance in Western society. Andy Brown

Printed in Great Britain
by Amazon